BEHIND THE
AI MASK

BEHIND THE AI MASK

Protecting Your Business from Deepfakes

CARL BOGAN

WILEY

To Lauren, for believing in the work even when I wasn't sure where it was heading.

Contents at a Glance

Contents

Introduction: The Deepfake Dilemma

In the not-so-distant past, the phrase "seeing is believing" was considered an unshakable truth. If something appeared on a screen, whether it was a photograph, a video, or a live broadcast, it was accepted as evidence. Visual and auditory cues carried an almost sacred credibility, forming the foundation of trust in our digital world. But that foundation has been shaken to its core. We now live in an era where technology has advanced to the point of crafting hyper-realistic illusions that can mimic reality so convincingly that they challenge even the most discerning human eye.

Welcome to the world of deepfakes.

Deepfakes (a portmanteau of "deep learning" and "fake") are images, videos, or audio that have been edited or generated using artificial intelligence, AI-based tools, or AV editing software. They may depict real or fictional people and are considered a form of *synthetic media,* which is media usually created by artificial intelligence systems by combining various media elements into a new media artifact.

Deepfake technology, powered by AI, represents a seismic shift in how we create, perceive, and interact with media. At its best, it is a tool of unparalleled creativity, a medium for resurrecting historical figures, de-aging actors, or crafting unforgettable moments of humor and artistry. At its worst, it is a weaponized force, capable of eroding trust, spreading disinformation, and exploiting human vulnerabilities on an unprecedented scale.

This book is about the double-edged sword of deepfakes. It's about their promise and their peril. It's about how this technology can make us laugh, cry, and marvel, and how it can make us doubt, fear, and question everything we know to be true. But most importantly, this book is about understanding what's at stake and how we can take action to navigate this rapidly changing landscape.

Imagine waking up to a video of a world leader declaring war, only to find out hours later that the video was a fabrication. Imagine a parent receiving a frantic phone call from their child, begging for help, only to discover it was a deepfake scam designed to extort money. Picture a CEO authorizing a multimillion-dollar wire transfer because they were deceived by the synthetic voice of their supposed superior. These aren't hypothetical scenarios; they've already happened.

Deepfakes thrive in the intersection of trust and technology. They exploit the very qualities that make us human: our instinct to trust familiar faces and voices, our emotions, and our need for connection. And as the technology becomes more sophisticated and accessible, its potential for harm grows exponentially.

But deepfakes are not inherently evil. They are a reflection of the intentions behind them. Just as fire can cook a meal or destroy a forest, deepfakes are tools: tools that demand ethical guidance and responsible use. For every scam and malicious actor, there are countless innovators using this technology to push the boundaries of storytelling, education, and art. The question isn't whether deepfakes are good or bad; the question is what we, as a society, will do with this power.

My journey into the world of deepfakes began with curiosity and a dash of mischief. In 2019, I was experimenting with this nascent technology late at night, fueled by little more than an overclocked GPU, a cup of coffee, and a wild idea to merge two cultural icons into one surreal mashup. The result, a deepfake of Cardi B and Will

Smith, went viral, racking up millions of views and sparking count-less conversations. What started as a fun experiment quickly became a career-defining moment. People couldn't stop sharing the clip, and even the celebrities themselves reacted with laughter and awe.

But as the views climbed and the headlines rolled in, a nag-ging thought crept into my mind: *What if this technology fell into the wrong hands?* If I could use it to create joy and laughter, couldn't someone else just as easily use it to deceive or harm? That realiza-tion was the turning point, the moment I understood that deepfakes weren't just a quirky technological trick; they were Pandora's box, opened wide for the world to see.

Over the years, I've used deepfakes to entertain millions, collabo-rate with major brands, and explore the boundaries of what's possible in visual storytelling. But I've also dedicated myself to understanding their darker implications—how they can be weaponized, how they exploit trust, and how they challenge the very fabric of reality. This dual perspective has shaped my philosophy: technology is neutral, but its impact depends entirely on how we wield it.

At its core, the deepfake dilemma is about trust. Trust in the media we consume, in the voices we hear, and in the institutions that govern our lives. Deepfakes don't just manipulate pixels; they manipulate perception. And when perception is compromised, trust becomes collateral damage.

Beyond being a technological issue, it's also a societal one. The erosion of trust has far-reaching consequences, from political desta-bilization to financial fraud to personal trauma. When we can no longer believe what we see or hear, the ripple effects touch every aspect of our lives.

But this book isn't about doom and gloom. It's about solutions. It's about empowering readers, whether you're a business leader, a policymaker, or an everyday citizen, to navigate the challenges and opportunities posed by deepfakes. It's about education, innovation, and collaboration. And yes, it's about having a few laughs along the way, because sometimes humor is the best antidote to fear.

In the pages ahead, you'll discover:

- How deepfakes work and the surprising psychology behind why they fool us
- Real-world stories of deepfake misuse, from corporate scams to viral hoaxes
- The ethical dilemmas and legal gray areas surrounding this technology
- Proactive solutions, including innovative tools, regulatory frameworks, and practical tips to protect yourself and your organization
- A vision for a future where deepfakes are used responsibly, fostering creativity and trust instead of chaos and deception

Deepfakes are here to stay. The question is not whether they will shape our future but how. This book is both a warning and a call to arms. It's a guide for navigating the complexities of this new reality, a rallying cry for ethical innovation, and a reminder that the choices we make today will define the digital landscape of tomorrow.

So, let's dive in. Let's explore the good, the bad, and the banana-flavored absurdity of deepfakes. Let's confront the challenges head-on, armed with knowledge, humor, and a commitment to doing what's right. Because the future of trust, and the future of reality itself, is in our hands.

Welcome to *Behind the AI Mask: Protecting Your Business from Deepfakes*. Let's get started.

BEHIND THE
AI MASK

Chapter 1

The Birth of Myster Giraffe: The Spark That Lit the Fire

The year 2019 was like handing a baby a blowtorch: chaotic, fascinating, and absolutely dangerous. Deepfake technology was creeping into public consciousness, lurking in corners of the Internet where most people feared to tread. The few clips floating around social media were crude, glitchy, and deeply uncanny, yet utterly hypnotic.

Every time I saw one, I clicked Replay. These early deepfakes weren't perfect, but that was part of their charm. They warped your sense of reality just enough to make you question what you were looking at, and that cognitive dissonance was addictive.

I had heard whispers about a repository named DeepFaceLab, an open-source deepfake tool buried deep in GitHub. It was one of the first publicly available tools that allowed users to experiment with AI-driven face replacement, setting the foundation for what would eventually become a revolution in synthetic media. It was a Frankenstein's monster of different scripts held together by batch files and sheer willpower. The documentation was nearly unreadable and poorly translated from Russian, but it was all we had.

For someone without a computer science background, using it felt like trying to assemble a crashed alien spacecraft missing half the parts with instructions written in a dead language. Every step was a mix of guesswork and trial and error, with moments of progress often undone by the next unexpected glitch. The first attempts were laughably bad: warped faces, flickering eyes, and lips that moved like rubber.

At the same time, I was working as Chief Technology Officer (CTO) at Aliza, a startup focused on building AI-powered digital influencers. My role involved leading the tech effort while pushing the boundaries of AI-driven character animation, but I quickly grew frustrated by the limitations. Traditional animation was expensive and time-consuming, requiring a large team of highly skilled artists to achieve impressive results. Additionally, the AI zeitgeist was barely beginning to progress, which meant the available AI tools lacked the realism we needed. That frustration, mixed with my growing obsession with deepfake technology, pushed me to start experimenting outside of work.

We worked out of a small office space on the west side of Los Angeles. As is the case at most startups, everyone wore many hats. At times I felt like I was in charge of anything that plugged into the wall. I built the servers, set up the local network, built the computers, maintained the server, and backed it up—and when things broke, I fixed them. The gear wasn't bleeding edge, but fortunately I knew the value of a good GPU.

There was a whiteboard across from my desk that slowly became covered in notes, scratch diagrams, and what I called "Roomba Method" loops. The room was warm from the constant hum of purpose-built workstations. Ken, a financial wizard with a killer instinct, logic, and reasoning, sat within arm's reach. We didn't speak the same visual language, as he was more comfortable daydreaming about Excel spreadsheets, but we clicked. Every day I'd come up with a new batch of ideas to bounce off of him, and somehow we'd puzzle through them together.

During the day I was trying to crack what seemed like a tough yet solvable puzzle, but more than that, I wanted to prove something. Deepfake technology and its techniques were the untested newbies compared to legacy software providers. For years, I watched software come and go, dismissed by industry incumbents and professionals alike as either passing trends or not production quality. With deep-fake, I immediately saw its potential as an art form and a new way to tell stories and challenge perceptions. No need for the multimillion-dollar pipeline and decades of experience to achieve semi-realism. That's when I started working on a side project—something with no rules, no corporate constraints, just me, pushing the technology as far as I could. This was the true birth of *Myster Giraffe*.

For days, I had been mulling over how to push my deepfake experiments to the next level. Every attempt felt like it was missing something—something that would make it more than just a technical exercise. Then, one day, inspiration struck.

The idea came when I wondered what would happen if I mashed together two wildly different cultural icons: people who, on the surface, had nothing in common, yet shared an underlying charisma. This wasn't just about combining faces; it was about exploring the hidden threads that connected seemingly unrelated personalities. That thought led to my first public-facing experiment with deepfake technology.

I spent hours tweaking neural networks, curating datasets, and running A/B tests with my *Roomba Method*, which is something I've developed over the years that allows me to analyze the bounds of a problem when I don't have enough information. It's similar to a known cybersecurity technique called the *brute-force method*, which involves systematically trying all possible solutions until the correct solution is found. Perhaps the main difference is that I combine the brute-force method with logical reasoning and understanding that allows for faster discovery. The first attempts were disasters: flickering eyes, faces that melted into digital nonsense. But after countless late nights, I hit gold.

The result was a surreal mashup of pop culture icon Will Smith and hip-hop artist Cardi B that felt like a fever dream (see Figure 1.1). It was funny, absurd, and oddly captivating. I uploaded it to social media and clicked Publish. The Internet exploded.

Figure 1.1 The deepfake mashup that launched Myster Giraffe
Source: Generated with AI usingCustom AI Software – AIMultiple

Scan to watch the video that started it all.

That's getting ahead of myself, though. Initially, I shopped it around internally, as we were courting Cardi B as a brand partner. "Perhaps we could show her as a measure of good faith that we had the best technology, that we were future-forward thinkers?" No one seemed to see the value in what I had just created. I could almost feel the chip forming on my shoulder. I thought to myself, "Is no one seeing this opportunity as clearly as I am? This is a big deal! I can see the next three to five years." It felt like a golden opportunity afforded to few, and one too heavy to ignore.

I uploaded it to the r/deepfake subreddit to get some measured feedback from known cynics. If you want to know whether your creation has legs, upload it to Reddit, and they'll let you know with zero hesitation. I received lukewarm feedback, but they didn't tear it apart. Success.

I hastily created an Instagram account and then began silently pondering in my head, "What's my angle? How do I want to be perceived? What's an animal people know the least about? Giraffes. Definitely giraffes. Oh wait, what if I was mysterious? People *love* mystery, I mean . . . Banksy, Daft Punk, Marshmallow, right? Ok, I'll be *mystergiraffe*." Boom, uploaded. Silence. For hours.

Aliza was working within Bam Labs, run by Brian Lee and his partners. We had just moved to a new office on the west side of Los Angeles, where we shared an office space with Brian. Brian had a wonderful assistant named Heidi. I showed Heidi my new creation in passing, and, as fate would have it, Heidi was a family friend of Will Smith's Family. She offered to post it to her account, where it would be visible to some of the other Smith family members. I excitedly took her up on the offer and forgot about it.

Within hours, the video went viral. Millions of views. Shares from Cardi and Will. Major outlets and blogs picked it up. And then the ultimate validation: Will Smith posted the video with the caption, "Whoever did this is hired."

For a brief, shining moment, I was riding the wave of viral, Internet-borne fame. People loved it, and no one knew who was behind it. In that moment, Myster Giraffe entered the realm of viral anonymity.

The majority of the feedback was lighthearted comments like "This is hilarious" and variations of delight, with a handful of detailed critiques from other digital creators and tech enthusiasts. Some pointed out technical flaws I had missed, such as unnatural eye movements, inconsistent lighting, or subtle artifacts that disrupted the illusion. Others provided suggestions for refining facial expressions and improving lip-sync accuracy, having no idea how I created it—classic Internet. All in all, this feedback loop became invaluable, pushing me to fine-tune my process and explore new techniques I wouldn't have considered on my own.

> The biggest lessons from going viral? Deepfakes aren't inherently good or bad; it's all about intent.

After my personal shock had reached a manageable level, I realized I had stumbled on the perfect way to refine my craft. Each subsequent viral video became an opportunity to test a new technique or feature of the software I was learning and experimenting with. It was like having a global focus group at my fingertips, with millions of people reacting to my work in real time. Although I'd already had a substantial career as a seasoned computer graphics/visual effects artist, deepfakes were an entirely new frontier. Social media became my barometer, offering unfiltered, immediate feedback that was both brutally honest and invaluable.

But as I basked in the glow of that first viral hit, an unsettling thought crept in:

What if someone used this technology for harm?

At first, it was just a nagging thought in the back of my mind; but as I saw more people reacting to my deepfakes, some laughing and others questioning their authenticity, I began to understand the true weight of what I had created. The same tool that entertained could also deceive, mislead, or manipulate. What started as a fun, creative outlet was beginning to feel like uncharted territory, with implications I hadn't fully grasped yet.

The VFX Artist Behind the Mask

Before this crazy moment, my months and years were spent jumping from post-production studio to commercial shoots across Los Angeles. I was a freelance VFX artist living in the commercial world, not because I had an aversion to film production, but because I enjoyed the freedom of consistently having to solve different types of problems while working on different projects every three to five weeks. I loved the pace of advertising. Fast turnarounds. Fresh briefs. A chance to reset often. I began my career working on Hollywood movie trailers, making whimsical titles and interstitials before migrating into game cinematics and high-polish capture. Over the years, I managed to experience nearly every corner of the CG landscape.

I lived and breathed the tools of the trade. Not in a collector's sense, but in a utilitarian, "solve-it-or-else" kind of way. Cinema 4D, Maya, 3ds Max, multiple tracking and compositing software packages—I picked them up and discarded them as needed. My philosophy was simple: if it helped me do my job better, I'd learn it. I wasn't waiting for permission. Looking back, that mindset led to a natural, almost inevitable conclusion—that I'd reach for machine learning when it came knocking.

My early "machine learning" experiments, which is what it was called before everything became "AI," were crude and clumsy, but a single test among the many during this phase changed everything. I attempted to turn my coworker, Xander, into visibly angry Judge Brett Kavanaugh (played by Matt Damon in a very funny SNL skit about the hearing with the Senate Judiciary Committee, during which Judge Kavanaugh is very upset with the entire process). With just 500 images, laughably small for a training dataset at the time, I began seeing strange results. Every time Xander said an *F* sound, a literal hole would appear in Xander's generated mouth. I couldn't explain it, but I knew it meant something. After thinking about this for a bit, I posited that we were missing the mouth shapes, or phonemes, that we needed to fill in the gap. I pulled out my phone and shot a short video of Xander saying 10 to 15 *F*-heavy words: French fries, fire, fantastic, and the more colorful ones, too. After adding the clip to the dataset and retraining, miraculously the hole vanished.

7

That was it. The aha moment. The realization that *data is gold*. Not algorithms. Not hardware. Data. It wasn't about hoping for results; it was about *teaching* the machine *what* to learn.

The road from there to Cardi Smith was fast and strange and hotter than I expected.

Myster Giraffe started not as a shield but as a stage. I understood that anonymity was a gimmick, yes, but a powerful one. People love novelty, yet they're also drawn to mystery. I wanted that mystique. It wasn't just a name. It was a character. A digital magician. That's why I spelled it *M-Y* instead of *M-I*. Like a misdirection.

And when "Cardi Smith" exploded, the first call I got wasn't from a fan. It was from the Aliza CEO, Brian Lee, the mind behind Legal-Zoom, Shoe Dazzle, and The Honest Company. He wasn't laughing. He was concerned. "Are we going to get sued?" he asked. I promised him we wouldn't and that I knew where the line was. He let it go. That moment scared me a little, but it also validated everything I knew Myster Giraffe could be.

So I slowed down . . . briefly. Then I floored it.

Because I could see what was coming. And I knew what the future would look like with Myster Giraffe in it.

The Super Deepfake Squad

While Myster Giraffe was gaining traction, I was still refining my craft, constantly searching for ways to push the limits of what was possible. My early deepfakes were compelling, but I knew there was room for improvement, especially in dataset curation and upscaling, two areas that weren't well-documented at the time. Then, after another viral creation, I received an invitation that pulled me into a whole new orbit: a secretive online collective known as the Super Deepfake Squad.

This wasn't just a casual Reddit group or a loose-knit 4chan channel. The Squad was a global gathering of the top deepfake creators, people who lived and breathed this technology. It was invite-only, and new members had to be unanimously approved. You couldn't just be good; you had to bring something unique to the table.

Inside, I found a mix of technical brilliance, creative audacity, and an overwhelming sense that we were all playing with something much bigger than ourselves. Imagine a group of people who had independently built rockets, finally meeting at the same launchpad. That was the Squad.

Joining the Squad wasn't just an invitation to an elite club; it was a fast track to knowledge that would have taken me years to figure out on my own. These were the people setting the pace for the entire field, and suddenly I was in the room.

What set me apart was my ability to tell a story with deepfakes. While others were focused purely on technical advancements, I was blending pop culture with emerging technology in a way that connected with audiences on an emotional level. But from a technical standpoint, I was still catching up. One of the biggest takeaways from the Squad was learning how to properly curate datasets and upscale imagery for cleaner, more convincing deepfakes. Before this, I had been pulling images haphazardly, letting the AI do its best with the mess I fed it. After learning the Squad's methods, I applied those refinements to my next viral deepfake, and the difference was like night and day.

I also stood out in other ways. Most of the Squad members weren't from the United States. Many were anonymous, hiding behind Discord handles and burner accounts. I was one of the only Americans and one of only two people who came from a professional visual effects background. I was also the only Black creator in the group. That wasn't lost on me. Culturally, I brought something different to the table. I wasn't there just to win benchmarks or flex technical might, but more so to remix American pop culture. To speak the language of memes and movies, not machine learning papers.

That tension gave me an edge, but it also made me feel alone at times. I knew references others didn't. I saw creative angles that weren't obvious to them. And that meant I had to blaze my own path inside a space where few could follow.

Although the Squad thrived on groundbreaking innovation, it also demanded a serious reckoning with boundaries.

The group operated in a space that was as gray as it was cutting-edge. Most of us loosely agreed on broad ethical principles, but there were always questions about where the line should be drawn.

For example, most of us avoided outright malicious projects, like impersonating someone to commit fraud or creating disinformation to influence political outcomes. Those were clear red lines. But not everything was black and white.

Some members created content that leaned into moral ambiguity—projects that weren't inherently harmful but could easily be misunderstood or repurposed in the wrong hands. For example, one member created a series of deepfake videos placing historical figures in modern-day scenarios, like a world leader giving a speech about current events. Although the intention was purely artistic and thought-provoking, the realism of the videos sparked debates online about their authenticity. It highlighted how even content designed for creative exploration could be twisted or misinterpreted when removed from its original context. These were the kinds of things that made me pause and think: *Just because we can, does that mean we should?*

Personally, I had my own boundaries. I wasn't interested in creating content that could manipulate public opinion in political contexts, impersonate someone for monetary gain or fraudulent purposes, or exploit someone's likeness in a way that could harm their reputation.

For me, deepfakes were about creativity, not control. They were a tool for storytelling, humor, and exploring the surreal, not for deception or exploitation.

That said, the group as a whole was largely on the side of right. Most members were careful about what they created, aware of the potential for misuse. Although some dipped into ethically gray areas, it was rarely with malicious intent. Instead, it often stemmed from a desire to test boundaries, to see what was possible and where society's limits truly lay.

The dynamic within the Squad was fascinating. On one hand, it was a collaborative think tank where we shared cutting-edge techniques, tips, and insights. We tackled some of the hardest problems in deepfake technology together: optimizing GPU load to enhance performance; curating datasets meticulously because, as the old adage says, "Garbage in, garbage out"; and pushing for the highest possible resolution at a time when digital upscaling was still in its infancy. We also explored methods to speed up model training, using pretrained models to cut down the turnaround time from concept to execution. It felt like we were at the forefront of a technological revolution, each breakthrough building on the last. On the other hand, it was fiercely competitive. We were all watching each other's work, measuring success by the reactions it got online, driven by an unspoken challenge to outdo one another.

These breakthroughs weren't just theoretical; they were practical tools that elevated my craft and pushed my work to new heights. One major breakthrough was mastering dataset curation. Before, I had been working with messy, inconsistent image sets, leading to subpar results. After refining my approach based on what I learned from the Squad, I saw immediate improvements. The faces were cleaner, details sharper, and overall realism significantly improved. Another game-changer was *upscaling*, a technique that was still emerging at the time. Learning how to extract and enhance images properly meant I could create deepfakes that held up even under close scrutiny, making them more convincing than ever before.

One of the unique aspects of the Squad was its anonymity. But it also fostered an unsettling reality: without personal accountability, boundaries became more fluid, and ethical lines blurred. Most members didn't share their real names, locations, or faces. This anonymity allowed for a free exchange of ideas, but it also created a layer of tension. Without personal accountability, people sometimes felt emboldened to experiment in ways that pushed ethical boundaries.

I remember one discussion in particular. A member shared a project they were working on: a deepfake that juxtaposed speeches from Trump and Hitler, blending their rhetoric in a way that was both provocative and unsettling. It was edgy, designed to highlight the power of narrative manipulation through deepfakes. The technical execution was flawless, eerily seamless in its transitions, blurring the lines between historical context and modern political discourse. The group's reaction was split. Some praised the project as a bold artistic statement, pushing the boundaries of what deepfakes could convey. Others, including me, questioned the implications, especially how easily such content could be misinterpreted or weaponized in the wrong hands.

Moments like that reminded me of the duality of this technology. It wasn't just a tool; it was a force multiplier. And like any powerful tool, its legacy would depend entirely on how it was used.

My time in the Super Deepfake Squad was transformative. It pushed me to refine my craft at a rapid pace, but it also forced me to acknowledge the darker implications of deepfake technology. For all the groundbreaking discoveries we made, the ethical burden only grew heavier. As I applied what I had learned to Myster Giraffe, I began to see just how easily deepfakes could manipulate perception, and how fragile the boundary between entertainment and deception truly was. Deepfake technology amplified the impact of digital content in ways traditional tools never could. For example, a simple meme might generate laughs or provoke thought, but when enhanced with deepfake elements, like seamlessly swapping faces or manipulating voices, it could transcend language barriers, evoke stronger emotional reactions, and spread exponentially faster across social platforms. This ability to magnify influence made deepfakes both revolutionary and, at times, unsettling.

The Squad wasn't just a collective of creators; it was an accelerator for deepfake evolution. But all good things must come to an end. The group slowly dissolved—not officially, but it fizzled out with less and less engagement week by week. I believe we all came to the simultaneous realization that we had accomplished both personal and collective goals we set out for. Some of us went on to work for visual effects studios and production houses, and others of us ventured into other directions, still adjacent to deepfakes and AI.

The techniques I picked up—curating cleaner datasets, improving upscaling methods, and optimizing training times—directly impacted my work. Although Myster Giraffe remained its own entity, these refinements allowed me to push quality further, making my creations even more seamless and immersive.

But with that evolution came deeper ethical questions. And for all the breakthroughs we achieved, the most important lesson I learned was this: deepfakes aren't inherently good or bad. Their legacy is up to us. Throughout my journey, I saw how they could be tools for creativity, humor, and storytelling, but also instruments of deception and manipulation. The challenge isn't just about refining the technology: it's about defining the boundaries of its use. The dilemmas we debated in the Squad, from art to deception, are the same ones society will keep wrestling with as deepfakes get more advanced and accessible.

The Giraffe Who Knew Too Much

The idea for a 30-minute show didn't just appear out of thin air. It came from a single, unforgettable moment. One of those spine-tingling,

Scan to see the video that broke people's brains.

electric moments that only happen when absurdity and technology collide perfectly.

It started with *Steve the Stallion*.

I had superimposed Steve Harvey's face onto Megan Thee Stallion during her NPR Tiny Desk performance of "Big Ol' Freak." It was surreal, hilarious, and totally hypnotic. His caterpillar-like mustache sat proudly above a flawless 26-inch bustdown weave. The look was chaotic and uncanny, and I knew, before the clip even finished training, that this was going to be a hit. I felt it in my spine. That weird, unmistakable feeling when you've just made something that the Internet can't ignore.

I sent the video to Tiffany Haddish, a popular comedian. We connected after I honored her in her very own deepfake, where she became "His Royal Badness, The Purple One, and The High Priest of Pop": Prince. Because of that incredibly funny video, she invited me to meet in person on the set of *Kids Say the Darndest Things*, where she was filming and Steve Harvey had formerly hosted. I told her, "Hey Tiffany. Would you mind getting my new video to Steve? I'm not sure if you know each other, but I have a feeling you do. :)" She immediately reposted it to her 6 million followers, and everything lit up. Twitter. Instagram. Blogs. Websites. Comments flying in from every direction. People didn't just laugh; it broke their brains. They *believed it*. It was too ridiculous to be real and too real to ignore.

Then it reached Steve's team.

They reached out. At first, they were a little standoffish. They said they could get it removed from Instagram if they wanted to—a flex, I guess, more than a threat. But I stayed cool. We talked it through. They explained how busy Steve was, but told me he saw it, and that it made him laugh. Which was the whole point. He's a comedian, after all.

That's when they mentioned something interesting. Steve wanted to launch a new segment on his show where he'd tell stories from his past and narrate them. Perhaps I wanted to take a swing at pitching what that would look like? It sounded like a solid opportunity. Maybe even a foot in the door. But deep down, I knew it wasn't the door I wanted to walk through.

Because I had already seen the bigger picture.

The reaction to Steve the Stallion proved something I had been feeling for a while. Deepfakes could be more than satire or one-off gags. They could be vessels for alternate realities. Not just "what if this celebrity said that," but "what if this entire cultural moment happened *differently?*"

I grew up watching shows like *Martin*, where Martin Lawrence invented characters like Sheneneh, and *In Living Color*, where Jamie Foxx transformed into Wanda. These weren't just impressions. They were full-blown personas. Entire worlds spawned from performance and imagination. I thought, why not do that, but with the ability to actually *see* those alternate realities unfold?

So I started assembling a team. With the help of a former talent agent from WME (William Morris Endeavor), an Emmy-winning producer, and a few creative allies, we built a pitch for a show starring Myster Giraffe: an interdimensional, culture-savvy giraffe who interviews celebrities not about what they're promoting, but about who they could have been, who they might still become, and what it means to be themselves across time and space.

We called it a mix of *Space Ghost Coast to Coast, Interdimensional Cable (from Rick and Morty)*, and *A Christmas Carol*. Deepfakes would power the individual segments, transporting guests into surreal, comedic, and thought-provoking alternate versions of themselves. A universe where Snoop Dogg became an anti-weed activist. A timeline where Tracee Ellis Ross was the moral center of the Huxtable universe. A future where our guests learn new skills, explore second acts, and talk to themselves across dimensions.

We pitched it to six different studios. We had Ron Funches attached. The documents were tight. The concept was polished. But nothing quite stuck. Maybe it was too early. Maybe we were bad at pitching. Maybe both. You never really find out.

What I do know is this: that pitch was a warning shot. A creative artifact from a future that was coming faster than anyone realized. We weren't just trying to sell a show. We were asking the industry to take synthetic media seriously *before it got serious*.

They all passed.

And now here we are.

But even with the industry watching, I wasn't done testing the limits, especially around stories that mattered to me.

There was one deepfake that still stands out as the most controversial thing I've ever made. Maybe the most important, too. Rapper Boosie Badazz had gone after Lil Nas X online, saying some pretty vile things about his sexuality. Everyone knew it crossed a line. So I asked a question: what if Boosie had been born gay? What if the roles were reversed?

I took Boosie's face and swapped it into a steamy, hypersexualized video that originally featured Lil Nas X. It was blurred, suggestive, and designed to hit hard. Not as revenge. As a mirror. The idea was simple: be kind, because this could have been you.

The response was electric. Some people applauded the message. Someone even invited Myster Giraffe to a gallery opening in NYC to converse about new media and how the landscape is changing. Others were furious. I got warned that Boosie might send people after me. I braced for the backlash that never quite came. That clip sat right on the line, maybe even over it, but I was willing to take the risk. I knew what I was doing. I wasn't trolling. I was trying to tell a story. One rooted in empathy, even if the packaging made people uncomfortable.

Every time I created a narrative-driven piece, I got that nagging feeling: Would they get it? Was I clear enough? Would people care?

Sometimes they did. Sometimes they didn't.

But once I posted it, I was glued to the comments. My hands would sweat. I turned my desktop volume up so I could hear the "ding" of new notifications like sonar pings in a submarine. That's how I knew something was catching. It was like a ritual. I'd finish the edit, write a tight caption, tag a few people directly, and hit publish.

Then I'd wait. Not for approval, but for impact.

That show may never have aired, but it lives in the DNA of everything I've done since. The concept of using deepfakes to entertain, to reflect, to *reimagine* the world instead of distorting it—that's still the mission. And maybe, just maybe, the next time the industry calls, they'll be ready for the future I saw back then.

But while Hollywood hesitated, I didn't. I needed to see what this tech could really do . . . live, unfiltered, and face to face.

Real-Time Deepfakes: The Turning Point

With the knowledge gained from the Squad and the technical advancements I was making at Aliza, I was eager to push deepfake technology further. But this time, I wasn't just experimenting. I needed to test its real-world application. And what better proving ground than a live Zoom job interview?

There's a moment every creator experiences when their work stops being just an experiment and starts feeling like something out of science fiction. For me, that moment came when I realized I could manipulate reality in real time. No more pre-rendered clips or post-production tricks. This was instantaneous, seamless, and transformative. I could become anyone, anywhere, at the push of a button.

We had retooled DeepFaceLab from the ground up in PyTorch at Aliza, making it leaner, faster, and optimized for real-time performance. I ran it on a custom-built Ubuntu Linux box with 128 gigabytes of RAM and an RTX 3090 GPU. My webcam was a Logitech Stream-Cam running at 30 fps, piped into the deepfake overlay. The visuals were clean, but lighting was everything. I used a large ring light to eliminate shadows on my face; the more even the light, the better the blend between my actual face and the identity I was borrowing.

The meeting was scheduled for early morning, but not by chance. Morning light poured through my home office windows and played nice with the system. Less harsh contrast meant fewer harsh shadows. I sat back from the camera slightly, making sure the angles worked. I cleaned up the background and placed a few subtle distractions in view—something eye-catching but not suspicious. I wanted just enough noise to keep their attention from locking too tightly on my face.

Then came the facial calibration. I'd smile to test how wide I could laugh before the facial tracking broke. I'd practice blink speed. I'd push my eyebrows to their limits. This wasn't just a technical test, but more of a performance rehearsal. I needed to know exactly where the boundaries were before stepping into the virtual meeting room.

No last-minute glitches. No backup plan. It was just me, Sinatra's face, and a Zoom link. The lights were perfect. The tech was humming. And I was about to walk into a meeting as someone else.

Naturally, I needed to see just how convincing it was. And what better test than fooling the experts trying to catch people like me in the act?

The company I was interviewing with was working on deepfake detection technology. Its mission? To spot manipulated media and label it as fake before it could do harm. In other words, the entire business revolved around catching people like me in the act.

Challenge accepted.

I decided to go big. For this interview, I didn't just want to show off my deepfake skills; I wanted to become a legend. So I picked Frank Sinatra. Why Sinatra? Partly because he's one of my favorite 1960s crooners, and partly because the sheer absurdity of "Ol' Blue Eyes" answering tech questions in 2020 was too good to resist. There was something magical about the idea of Sinatra talking GPUs and neural networks—two worlds colliding in a way no one could've imagined.

Now, I know what you're thinking: "Wouldn't the interviewer recognize Frank Sinatra's face?" That's a very astute question. However, without drilling down too deeply into the technical aspects, replacing the interior of one face with another while maintaining likeness has more to do with the similarities of facial and jaw shape than your actual facial features. Amazing, right? It isn't an obvious fact, but as far as the tech is concerned, the better the match of the jaw shape, the better the likeness match.

The setup was simple but nerve-wracking. Before the call, I configured my real-time deepfake dataset to map Sinatra's face onto mine. Every expression, every blink, every subtle movement—it all had to sell the illusion. I practiced in front of my webcam, fine-tuning every detail until it felt as natural as putting on a pair of sunglasses. When the Zoom call started, I was Sinatra.

I nodded, smiled, and answered their questions to the best of my ability. The interviewer didn't flinch. Not once. He asked about my experience, my process, and my thoughts on the future of AI, and I responded with the kind of confidence you'd expect from someone who ran the Rat Pack. It wasn't just about fooling him, it was about inhabiting the role. I made eye contact with the webcam (but not too much; nobody trusts a starer). I gestured naturally. I threw in a few quips to keep it light. The entire time, I was thinking: How does this look on the other side? Is it holding up? And then, the moment of truth.

As the interview wrapped up, I leaned in and said, "Hey, I just wanted to let you know, this isn't my real face." The pause that followed was delicious. At first, the interviewer looked confused, like he had misheard me. But then I turned off the deepfake overlay and revealed my actual face (see Figure 1.2).

I'll never forget his reaction. His jaw dropped, his face turned bright red, and he stammered as his brain tried to process what had just happened. You could almost see the error message flashing in his eyes: Does not compute. Does not compute. When he finally spoke, it was a mix of disbelief and delight. "Wait, how did you do that? How is this even possible?!" The kicker? This was his business! The company was building tools to detect exactly this kind of thing, and he had been completely fooled.

Figure 1.2 Real-time deepfake technology demonstrates seamless face replacement in live video calls
Source: Generated with AI usingCustom AI Software – AIMultiple

The goal was to quietly expose a company whose mission was to detect fake media, and I had achieved my goal. Why did it work? The company didn't know what it didn't know. It was focused on being reactive rather than proactive. I'm not even sure if the company knew this was a possibility at the time.

Within 48 hours, I had a job offer, which I declined. The company wanted me on the team immediately in an operations role. But although the success of the experiment was thrilling, it also left me with a deep sense of unease.

If I could do this in real time, what was stopping someone else from using this technology maliciously? What if a CEO was impersonated to authorize a fraudulent wire transfer? What if a political figure was framed in a fake video? The possibilities were endless, and not in a good way. This was a very cool trick, but it became something else entirely moments later. It was a fundamental challenge to authenticity, trust, and identity.

Looking back, the Sinatra experiment was a turning point in my deepfake journey. It wasn't just about proving what was possible; it was about realizing the implications of what I had created. In that Zoom call, I saw the future. A future where anyone could be anyone, where reality was malleable, and where the line between fact and fiction was razor thin.

But that responsibility wasn't just theoretical. It was staring me in the face. If I could fool an expert trained to detect deepfakes, what did that mean for the general public? What did that mean for the future of trust itself? The same technology that could make people laugh could also destroy trust. And that's when I

> Deepfakes aren't just tools, they're mirrors. They reflect our intentions, our values, and, ultimately, the world we want to create.

knew: if I was going to keep exploring this space, I had to do it ethically, with a clear set of principles guiding every decision.

Trust Experiments: The Kevin Calls

If anything, the Sinatra test only made me more curious. I didn't retreat. I sped up. I started to think: What happens when this technology leaves the lab? What happens when it's not just a proof of concept, but a social weapon?

That's when I began what I called the *trust experiments*. I gave myself a new identity: Kevin. A calm, friendly, inoffensive guy with questions about life. And I started making phone calls, real-time deepfaked video calls, wearing Frank Sinatra's face.

I'd tell a friend, "Hey, I want to test something. Can I talk to your spouse real quick?" They knew exactly what I was doing, and I made sure they were on board before anything started. They would prime their partners in advance, letting them know a friend was going to ask some questions, but not giving away the full context. That way, when I showed up on screen as Kevin, the door was already open. They'd hand over the phone or laptop, and suddenly I was Kevin. I wore a hoodie. I changed my voice. I dimmed the lights just enough. The goal was simple: could I keep someone talking long enough that they wouldn't question the face in front of them?

And it worked.

The trick was distraction. I'd lead with a topic I knew they cared about. A passion. A career goal. Something that would make them talk. Once they started, it was a waterfall. I'd nod, encourage them, drop in a few "mm-hmms," and let them talk for 10 minutes straight. They never questioned who I was, mainly because someone they trusted had handed me off. That social pass, that cosign, was everything (see Figure 1.3).

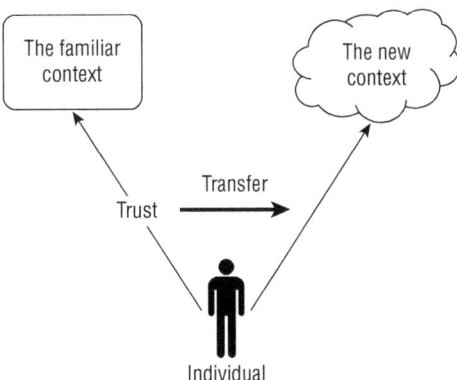

Figure 1.3 The trust transfer effect: how deepfakes exploit social verification chains

I did this at least a dozen times with different friends and family members. Sometimes it was Sinatra. Other times I tried Steve Harvey, complete with a fake voice, a suit, and the signature hat. The impression wasn't great, so the Harvey calls never went very far. But that didn't matter. What mattered was that even a weak impersonation could hold water for just long enough to be dangerous.

Each call taught me something new about human behavior—how quickly we fill in gaps, how eager we are to believe what feels familiar. It wasn't about technical perfection. It was about social engineering.

I wasn't catfishing. I wasn't manipulating anyone's emotions. But I was watching the machinery of trust bend in real time. And that realization hit harder than any hardware flex ever could.

Audience Reactions and Social Media Psychology

Every deepfake I released wasn't just about the technology; it was a test of human perception, a way to see how people processed reality in an era where the lines between real and artificial were becoming increasingly blurred. I wasn't just testing neural networks. I was testing how people's brains processed reality itself. Social media became my real-time laboratory, a place where I could observe, in vivid detail, how people responded to the blurring line between truth and fabrication.

At first, I assumed the audience would always be able to tell the difference between real and fake. Early deepfake videos were crude, filled with glitches and inconsistencies that made them easy to spot. Even when my own work started improving, I still believed that people's critical thinking would override any potential confusion. That belief didn't last long. The responses followed a predictable arc. Some people were immediately confused, staring at the clip, trying to process whether or not it was real. Others laughed, entertained by the absurdity of what they were watching. But then there were those who experienced something deeper: a slow, creeping unease, as if realizing for the first time that their eyes and memories could be tricked.

The most unsettling realization came when people began to misremember things that had never happened. Human memory is malleable, easily influenced by suggestion and repeated exposure. When people saw a deepfake enough times, it wasn't just fooling them in the moment; it was altering their recollection of the past. I once deepfaked a famous musician into an old movie scene, a lighthearted mashup meant to entertain. But soon, people in the comments weren't just reacting to it. They were debating whether they had actually seen it before. Some swore they had. Others even claimed to remember details from a version of the film that never existed. This is also what's known as the *Mandela Effect,* which is a phenomenon where a group of people share a consistent false memory of an event, historical fact, or detail. Was I creating mental illusions at scale with the aid of social media?

It wasn't just about creating viral content anymore; it was about realizing the responsibility that came with it. If people could misremember something as harmless as a movie scene, what else could deepfakes rewrite? What if bad actors leveraged this technology to alter history in ways far more dangerous? The implications were staggering, and I could feel the weight of what I had unleashed. It meant that deepfakes weren't just deceiving people in real time; they had the power to reconstruct memories. It wasn't just about fooling the eye. It was about rewriting history in people's minds.

That changed everything for me. Myster Giraffe had started as a playground for technical experiments, but suddenly, it had become something bigger. What started out as making funny and engaging viral content had become a study of how fragile human perception truly is.

Cancel Culture's Impact on Deepfake Comedy

Comedy has always thrived on pushing boundaries, but deepfake comedy introduced an entirely new level of risk. In traditional humor, exaggeration is key. An impressionist can distort a celebrity's voice; a cartoonist can stretch features into a caricature; a stand-up comedian can highlight absurd traits. But deepfakes? Deepfakes didn't just mimic. They became the person. And that raised serious ethical questions.

When I first started making deepfake comedy, I believed intent was the most important thing. If a joke was clearly harmless, then it should be fair game. But over time, I realized that intent doesn't matter when you're dealing with perception. It's not about what I meant; it's about how the audience interpreted it.

One particular deepfake taught me that lesson the hard way. It was a parody, obvious in its absurdity, or at least I thought so. What happens when Curtis "50 Cent" Jackson meets an obscure 1980s fitness enthusiast named Toni Britts, known for the catch phrase "That's it"? Toni was infamous for donning barely legal short shorts, but hey, it was the 80s, right? The Myster Giraffe secret recipe I was concocting at the time had some heavy ingredients of cognitive dissonance, which took the tough-guy persona of hip-hop artist 50 Cent, who is most famously known for being shot nine times and surviving, with a scantily clad fitness guru who moved his body as if he was a Pilates instructor merged with a belly dancer. But within hours, people who had missed the context were reacting as if it was something sinister. Some argued that even though the deepfake was clearly fake, it still had the potential to mislead those who didn't know better. That moment forced me to reconsider what I thought were hard lines between comedy and deception.

Deepfakes inherently blur those boundaries, and once they enter the public domain, they take on a life of their own. A well-intentioned joke, reposted out of context, could easily turn into something misleading or even harmful.

That raised even bigger ethical dilemmas. Was it okay to put someone's face on another person's body? Could deepfake comedy be considered a form of identity theft? What if a celebrity didn't find it funny? What if someone only saw the deepfake but never saw the explanation?

I developed my own set of rules to navigate these questions:

- Never mock the vulnerable.
- Never misrepresent someone's character.
- Make sure the subject of the deepfake could laugh along with it.

Those guidelines kept me grounded, but they didn't eliminate the risks.

Deepfake comedy wasn't just about technical skill anymore; it was about navigating an ever-shifting cultural minefield. I never considered myself to be a comedian, as I regard that title to be protected and held by the craftspeople who wield their words as such. However, in an era where online outrage could go viral just as fast as the content itself, every joke had to be considered from all possible angles.

The truth is, about 90 percent of what I've created will never see the light of day. By design, I set the bar of scrutiny for myself intentionally high. I might have an idea that's right on the line, which often gives birth to the best ideas, but sometimes I cross that line. And that's where I draw it. When something sounds good in my head but doesn't survive the transition to screen, I shelve it. It doesn't mean I delete it. It's still my art. But I've learned that just because I *can* post something doesn't mean I *should*.

A friend once told me, "Impact over intent." That stuck with me. As a creator, it doesn't matter what I meant to say if the message lands in a way that causes harm. Intent can't always shield you. It's the impact that lingers.

That philosophy became a filter for everything I made going forward. It shaped how I approached humor and how I balanced the thrill of pushing boundaries with the responsibility of holding that power in my hands. Humor has always been at the heart of Myster Giraffe, but it's a balancing act.

When you're playing with people's faces and their identities, you're not just making jokes. You're treading into the intimate corners of how they see themselves and how others see them. It's a line that can cut both ways.

I learned that lesson in the most direct way with the project that involved Lil Nas X and Boosie. It was the only time I stepped over the line on purpose. I knew the risk was worth it because the moment was so charged, so raw. But even then, I never forgot that the work I was doing had real consequences.

It's a line I've never taken lightly. There's an old saying: you shouldn't point a gun at someone unless you're ready to pull the trigger. With deepfakes, it's the same thing. If I'm going to take that shot, it had better come with solid reasoning. As a general rule of thumb, I'd rather make something that lifts people up than something that tears them down. That's why I'm so careful about how I use humor

The Birth of Myster Giraffe: The Spark That Lit the Fire

in my work. It's not about shock value or cheap shots. It's about finding that sweet spot where the audience can laugh, feel seen, and maybe even feel a little more connected to the world around them. Over time, that understanding of humor's power became part of a much bigger realization.

The Ethics of Viral Manipulation

Deepfakes represent control. Control over perception. Control over truth. Control over what people believe.

At first, I didn't think much about the ethical implications of what I was doing. Myster Giraffe had always been fun, bending reality enough to create something entertaining. But the more I experimented, the more I realized how much power I held.

As I discussed earlier regarding audience psychology, deepfakes can plant false memories and alter how people remember the past. When I realized that this power extended far beyond entertainment, everything changed for me.

I had always believed that deepfakes were tools that could serve good or bad purposes depending on the creator. But witnessing firsthand how easily perception could be manipulated and memories rewritten taught me something crucial: how people received and internalized what I created could matter more than what I originally intended.

This realization fundamentally shifted my approach. I still wanted to push boundaries, but I couldn't ignore the reality that deepfakes had evolved beyond an art form into something with genuine power to shape reality. And like any powerful tool, they demanded responsible use.

The weight of this responsibility became heavier with each viral success. Every share, every reaction, every comment that said "Wait, is this real?" reminded me that I was participating in a larger conversation about truth, authenticity, and trust in our digital age.

It forced me to ask harder questions: What happens when this technology becomes more accessible? What safeguards need to exist? How do we maintain a sense of shared reality when anyone can make anyone appear to say or do anything?

These had become practical challenges that I—and everyone working with synthetic media—would need to address. The technology was advancing faster than our collective understanding of its implications.

This ethical awakening didn't stop me from creating, but it made me more deliberate about what I chose to make and release. The playground was still there, but now it came with guardrails I had constructed for myself based on the real-world impact I had witnessed.

Lessons from Going Viral

Going viral is like an adrenaline rush mixed with a high-stakes gamble. When it first happened to me, I was chasing it—the views, the shares, the headlines, the reactions from celebrities. There was nothing like it. But over time, I realized that virality isn't just about gaining attention. It's about losing control. Once a deepfake went viral, it was no longer mine. People could repost it, misinterpret it, use it out of context, and twist it into something it was never meant to be. I had seen it happen to other creators; a single clip taken the wrong way could suddenly turn into a wildfire of controversy. I learned to be strategic. Virality wasn't the goal anymore; impact was. It wasn't about making something that got the most views. It was about making something that resonated for the right reasons.

The biggest lesson from going viral? Deepfakes aren't inherently good or bad. But intent doesn't matter when the impact spins out of your hands. People will always believe what they want, regardless

Once a deepfake is out in the world, it belongs to the Internet, not the creator.

of what's true. Once a deepfake is out in the world, it belongs to the Internet, not the creator. However, for me, ethical responsibility has always mattered more than engagement.

What's Next?

Myster Giraffe started as a joke, but by the time I had gone viral multiple times, it had become something far bigger than I could have imagined. It was about navigating a world where reality itself was bendable, remixable, and dangerously fragile. And as such, when the tech evolved, so did my responsibility. I had surpassed the point of making funny deepfake videos from alternate realities. Now, my friends . . . I was shaping perception.

But perception doesn't shape itself in a vacuum. It feeds on context—on what people know, what they assume, and what they were never taught to question. The next chapter looks outward, to a world that still thinks deepfakes are harmless fun or future problems. It explores how ignorance, at scale, became the perfect environment for deception to thrive. Because if you can't spot the trick, you never realize you've been fooled.

Chapter 2

Very Brief History of Synthetic Media

"You're probably wondering how we got here."

The technology I wielded as Myster Giraffe felt revolutionary, and it was, but the hustle was ancient. Every time I watched someone's face light up with wonder at a deepfake, every time I saw that moment of doubt flicker across their eyes ("Is this real?"), I was witnessing something that has played out for more than 150 years. The tools change, yet the human difficulty in determining real from fake remains constant.

Before we can understand how to defend against today's synthetic threats, we need to understand the hidden pattern. Because the finance worker who wired $25 million to fake executives in Hong Kong wasn't the first victim of manipulated reality. He was just the latest in a long line stretching back to grieving mothers in Boston parlors, paying good money to see their dead sons one more time.

The Analog Era (1870s–1980s): The First Deceptions

In April 1869, William Mumler stood trial for fraud in New York City, where he had fled from growing skepticism in Boston. Mumler claimed to take "spirit photographs" that showed the ghostly images of deceased loved ones appearing alongside living subjects, using double-exposure techniques to create what appeared to be supernatural encounters. The trial became a sensation that gripped the nation. The Mayor of New York himself had ordered an undercover investigation, sending Marshal Joseph H. Tooker to Mumler's studio posing as a customer. When Mumler photographed Tooker, and the resulting photo included a ghostly figure that Mumler claimed was Tooker's deceased father-in-law, the marshal had seen enough.

Mumler was arrested and charged with multiple counts: obtaining money through false pretenses, fraud, and larceny. The trial drew massive attention. The prosecution's star witness was none other than P.T. Barnum, the master showman who knew a humbug when he saw one. Barnum testified that he'd commissioned photographer Abraham Bogardus to create a fake spirit photograph showing Barnum with the ghost of Abraham Lincoln, demonstrating to the court exactly how such images could be fabricated through double exposure and other techniques.

The prosecution presented nine different methods by which Mumler could have faked his photographs. Expert photographers testified about techniques ranging from prepared plates to hidden accomplices. Former clients who'd been swindled spoke of recognizing their "deceased" relatives walking around Boston very much alive. The evidence seemed overwhelming.

But Mumler's defense was brilliant in its simplicity: prove it. Yes, there were many ways these photographs could be faked, but could anyone prove that Mumler had actually used any of them? When challenged to catch him red-handed (to expose his exposure, so to speak), the experts came up empty. Photographers who watched his every move, examined his equipment, and studied his plates found nothing. Mumler's defense was simple: "You say there are nine ways to fake this. Fine. Now prove I used any of them."

They couldn't.

The judge ultimately acquitted Mumler, not because he believed in spirit photography, but because the prosecution couldn't prove fraud beyond a reasonable doubt. The verdict was controversial; many saw it as a failure of justice that allowed a charlatan to continue preying on the grieving.

But here's what matters for our story: even after a trial that aired every possible method of photographic deception, even after P.T. Barnum himself showed how easy it was to fake a ghost, people kept buying spirit photographs. The public had just been given a master-class in photographic manipulation, and yet they lined up at Mumler's studio anyway.

It was after this trial, with Mumler's reputation both damaged and paradoxically enhanced by the publicity, that Mary Todd Lincoln visited his Boston studio in 1872. Using the false name "Mrs. Lindall," the former First Lady sat for what would become Mumler's most famous photograph, and her last. In the developed image, there appeared the unmistakable figure of Abraham Lincoln, hands resting on his widow's shoulders (see Figure 2.1).

People wanted to believe. The trial hadn't exposed Mumler's technique; it had only exposed humanity's willingness to pay for comforting illusions.

This is the pattern that would haunt us for the next 150 years. New technology creates a convincing deception. Experts expose the trick. People believe anyway.

Fast-forward to 1917. . .

. . .and we have what might be the most perfectly absurd case of mass expert delusion in history. Two young girls, Elsie Wright (16) and Frances Griffiths (9), were getting in trouble for constantly coming home with wet feet and muddy clothes after playing at a nearby stream called Cottingley Beck, near Bradford in England. When Frances's mother scolded her yet again, the girl insisted she kept going back to "see the fairies."

Figure 2.1 William Mumler's 1872 photograph of Mary Todd Lincoln with the "ghost" of Abraham Lincoln
Source: William H Mumler / Wikimedia Commons / Public domain

Her mother scoffed. So Elsie, who worked at a Bradford studio, retouching photographs, and considered herself something of an artist, hatched a plan. She borrowed her father's Midg quarter-plate camera (this was Elsie's first time taking a photograph, by the way), and the girls returned within an hour with "proof."

When Elsie's father Arthur developed the plate in his home darkroom, there was Frances, surrounded by dancing fairies (see Figure 2.2). Arthur Wright, a practical man and amateur photographer himself, immediately knew something was up. The proportions were wrong. The lighting was suspicious. His daughter knew photography tricks from her job. While the girls were out, he ransacked

Figure 2.2 Frances Griffiths with the "Leaping Fairy," 1917
Source: Elsie Wright / Wikimedia Commons / Public domain

their bedroom and searched the garden, looking for cardboard cutouts or any evidence of trickery.

He found nothing. Not because the girls were master criminals; they'd simply thrown away the evidence after each photo. But here's where it gets interesting: Arthur's wife Polly was a member of the Theosophical Society, and she believed. When she took the photographs to a Bradford Theosophical meeting in 1920, they eventually reached Edward Gardner, the society's general secretary.

Gardner didn't just believe; he went into overdrive. He had photography expert Harold Snelling examine the images. Snelling's verdict? "Entirely genuine," photographed "in a single exposure," showing "no trace whatever of studio work." Then Gardner did something remarkable: he had Snelling "clean up" the photographs to make them clearer. Yes, the expert who vouched for their authenticity was literally doctoring them to look more convincing.

Enter Sir Arthur Conan Doyle, creator of the world's most logical detective. In 1920, he was writing an article about fairies for *The Strand Magazine*'s Christmas edition when he heard about the photos. The timing seemed like destiny. Here was photographic proof arriving just when he needed it!

Doyle sent the photos to Kodak. The company's experts examined them meticulously and concluded that they couldn't find evidence of double exposure or trickery. But (and this is crucial) Kodak refused to certify them as genuine. The company essentially said, "We can't prove they're fake, but we're not saying they're real either." Gardner interpreted this as anti-Spiritualist bias. Doyle ignored the hesitation entirely.

The best part? When critics pointed out that the fairies looked suspiciously modern (one expert noted they had "very fashionable hairstyles," as if the supernatural beings were keeping up with 1917 fashion trends), Doyle dismissed it. When skeptics noted that Frances was looking at the camera instead of the miraculous fairies dancing in front of her, believers had an answer for that, too.

In July 1920, Doyle sent Gardner to investigate in person. Gardner found the Wright family "transparently honest and simple." He gave the girls new cameras: two W. Butcher & Sons Cameo folding plate cameras with secretly marked photographic plates to prevent tampering. The girls promptly produced three more fairy photographs.

When Doyle published his article "Fairies Photographed: An Epoch-Making Event" in the December 1920 *Strand Magazine*, it sold out within days. He wrote that these photos would "jolt the material twentieth-century mind out of its heavy ruts." He'd go on to publish an entire book, *The Coming of the Fairies*, in 1922.

The *Westminster Gazette* sent an investigative commissioner in January 1921. After extensive investigation, he couldn't definitively prove the photos were fake. The girls had created unbreakable rules: fairies only appeared to children, only when completely alone, only in good weather. No adult could verify independently.

Here's the kicker: Elsie had copied the fairy designs from *Princess Mary's Gift Book*, a 1915 children's book. She drew them on paper, added wings, and stuck them in the ground with hatpins. A "gnome" in their second photo was traced from an advertisement. The whole thing took them about 30 minutes per photo.

But they couldn't confess. As Elsie said decades later in 1985, "Two village kids and a brilliant man like Conan Doyle? Well, we could only keep quiet." Frances added, "I can't understand to this day why they were taken in. They wanted to be taken in."

Think about the cascade of expert failure here. Elsie's father, the only skeptic, was ignored. Snelling, the expert, not only validated the fakes but "improved" them. Kodak's technicians couldn't find proof of fakery in cardboard cutouts. Gardner, sent as an investigator, came back more convinced than before. Doyle, whose character Sherlock Holmes would have solved this in minutes, became the fairy fraud's biggest champion.

The hoax lasted 66 years. It wasn't definitively debunked until the 1980s, when Geoffrey Crawley from the *British Journal of Photography* proved that the fairies matched illustrations from the children's book. Even then, when the elderly women finally confessed in 1983, Frances insisted until her death that the fifth photograph (showing fairies without the girls) was real. She couldn't fully let go of the lie.

Now, here's why this matters for your business today: these weren't sophisticated manipulations. They were paper cutouts. With hatpins. Created by teenagers. Yet they fooled photography experts, Kodak technicians, investigative journalists, and one of the most famous logical minds of the era. Why? Because when people want to believe something badly enough, expertise becomes irrelevant.

The "experts" weren't analyzing evidence; they were confirming biases.

Sound familiar? Today's deepfakes don't need hatpins. They have neural networks. They don't fool grieving spiritualists seeking comfort after World War I. They fool finance directors authorizing wire transfers under false authority. The technology is infinitely more sophisticated, but the vulnerability is identical: when we want something to be true, we'll ignore every red flag screaming that it's not.

Replace "fairies" with "celebrity endorsements" and "cardboard cutouts" with "AI-generated videos," and you've got today's deepfake landscape. The tools evolved, but the exploit remained the same: our desperate need to trust what we see.

The Soviet Union transformed this vulnerability into state policy on an industrial scale. Joseph Stalin eliminated political rivals and then systematically erased them from history itself, employing an entire bureaucracy dedicated to rewriting the visual record.

Consider the most famous example: Nikolai Yezhov, chief of the secret police who oversaw Stalin's Great Purge from 1936 to 1938. In April 1937, Yezhov was photographed walking with Stalin along the Moscow-Volga Canal, a symbol of Soviet achievement. By 1940, after Yezhov himself was executed for "disloyalty," he had vanished from the photograph, replaced by more canal water. The man who had orchestrated the arrests and executions of 750,000 people during the Great Purge had himself been purged from existence. There's dark poetry in his being replaced by water, because he was also commissar of water transport.

But Yezhov was just one of many. David King, in his book *The Commissar Vanishes*, documented how "the physical eradication of Stalin's political opponents at the hands of the secret police was swiftly followed by their obliteration from all forms of pictorial existence."

The techniques were primitive: scalpels, airbrushes, darkroom chemicals, physical cutting and pasting. Photo retouchers spent long hours removing enemies while also smoothing Stalin's pockmarked complexion (from childhood smallpox), lengthening his withered left arm, and increasing his stature. Reality was negotiable at every level.

Take the 1922 photograph of Stalin with Lenin. This image appeared in every Soviet newspaper, showing them as comrades. But the photograph was fake, carefully crafted to give the impression that Stalin and Lenin were close friends, when they were anything but. Stalin had literally inserted himself into history as Lenin's chosen successor.

The scope was staggering. A 1926 photograph shows Stalin with party bosses Nikolai Antipov, Sergey Kirov, and Nikolai Shvernik. One by one, all except Stalin disappeared from the picture. After all the photo manipulations done through the years, Stalin stands alone.

Leon Trotsky, who founded the Red Army and stood beside Lenin during the Revolution, became Soviet history's greatest disappearing act. In a famous 1920 photograph at Moscow's Bolshoi Theater, Trotsky stands prominently beside the podium where Lenin addresses the troops. In later versions, Trotsky has vanished completely. The man who helped win the Revolution had been erased from it.

The manipulation went beyond subtraction; elements were added, too. A 1917 demonstration photograph was doctored so a shop sign reading "Clocks, Gold and Silver" became "You'll take what's yours through struggle," and an unreadable flag suddenly proclaimed "Down with the monarchy!" History was being rewritten to be more revolutionary than reality.

What made this particularly insidious was the participatory nature of the erasure. Soviet citizens practiced "personal responsibility" by scratching out faces from their own books and photographs. During the Great Purge, civilians would deface or destroy photographs containing images of those who had fallen from favor, fearing association with Stalin's enemies.

Think about that psychological operation: millions of people actively participating in rewriting their own memories. Children watching their parents carefully ink out faces from family photos. Students tearing pages from textbooks. Libraries destroying entire archives. The elimination of enemies required their very existence to be denied by everyone who had ever known them.

As Yale philosophy professor Jason Stanley notes in *How Propaganda Works*, "At the heart of authoritarian propaganda is the manipulating of reality." But Stalin understood something deeper: if you control the photographic record, you control memory itself. The constant manipulation created an atmosphere where citizens could never be sure what was real and what was fabricated. People began to question their own memories when confronted with contradictory "official" photographs.

The technical sophistication was remarkable for the predigital era. Stalin commissioned an army of painters to create official portraits, offering massive sums to artists. Then these portraits were reproduced and retouched over and over until they met his approval. Documentation on the retouching process was astounding in its detail, reflecting tremendous anxiety "lest something go awry."

By the 1940s, retouchers were manufacturing entire alternate realities. The famous photograph of Soviet soldiers raising the flag over the Reichstag in 1945? Later revealed to be staged and altered. Even victory needed editing.

The parallels to today are impossible to ignore, although the technology has evolved beyond Stalin's wildest dreams. Whereas Soviet retouchers needed weeks with scalpels and chemicals to erase a commissar, modern systems can rewrite reality in real time. Whereas

Stalin needed an army of artists to craft his image, today's tools can generate infinite variations instantly.

Consider how contemporary authoritarian regimes use these techniques. Protesters vanish from photographs of public squares. Crowds at political rallies multiply or shrink depending on the narrative. Inconvenient moments disappear from the record before most people even know they happened. The difference is speed and scale: what took Stalin's retouchers months now happens in microseconds, spreading globally before fact-checkers can respond.

Even more concerning is how this has been democratized. Stalin needed state resources to rewrite history. Today, anyone with a smartphone can alter reality. The same psychological vulnerabilities that allowed Soviet citizens to accept edited photographs now operate at a global scale, amplified by social media algorithms that reward engagement over accuracy.

We're watching the same cycle unfold: reality becomes negotiable, trust erodes, and people begin to doubt their own memories. When every image could be manipulated, when every video might be synthetic, we're all living in Stalin's darkroom. We just don't realize who's holding the scalpel anymore.

Meanwhile, Hollywood taught different lessons. Through matte paintings and optical printing, filmmakers created otherwise-impossible worlds. King Kong climbing the Empire State Building in 1933 wasn't real; everyone knew that. But in a darkened theater, it might as well have been. This consensual deception (we know it's fake but agree to believe) became the template for how we initially approached digital manipulation. We thought we could always tell the difference between entertainment and reality.

The 1967 Patterson-Gimlin Bigfoot footage proved otherwise. This grainy film of an alleged Sasquatch became the second-most-watched amateur footage in history, after the Zapruder film (the famous silent home-movie sequence shot by Abraham Zapruder that captured President John F. Kennedy's assassination in Dallas on November 22, 1963).

October 20, 1967. Two rodeo cowboys from Yakima, Roger Patterson and Bob Gimlin, are riding horses through Bluff Creek in Northern California, looking for Bigfoot. Patterson's got a 16 mm camera. They capture 59.5 seconds of footage, 954 frames total. In those frames, something walks across a sandbar, turns to look at them, and disappears into the woods.

Frame 352 is the money shot. The creature (they call her "Patty") looks directly at the camera over her shoulder. That single frame becomes the universal image of Bigfoot. You've seen it. Everyone's seen it. It's on t-shirts, documentaries, and beer labels.

Here's what makes this footage genius, whether real or fake: 55 years later, nobody's definitively proven it's fake. Not for lack of trying.

The analysis got obsessive. Professor Jeff Meldrum showed it to his anatomy students. They identified the trapezius, deltoid, erector spinae, shoulder blades moving under skin, quads contracting when they should. Frame by frame, believers mapped every muscle movement, every shadow, every footfall.

Meanwhile, skeptics had their ammunition. A costume manufacturer named Phillip Morris claimed he sold Patterson the suit. Bob Heironimus, a local guy, said he wore it. But their stories kept changing. The suit they produced looked nothing like Patty.

Meldrum compared Patty to the apes in *Beneath the Planet of the Apes*, state-of-the-art Hollywood costumes from the same era. His verdict: "They look like big hairy Pillsbury Doughboys." If Hollywood couldn't make a convincing ape suit with unlimited budgets, how did two broke cowboys from Yakima pull it off?

The footprints tell another story. The tracks show a pressure ridge from a flexible midfoot, something Meldrum has found in prints across decades and continents. You'd need to fake not just a costume but an entire anatomical system nobody knew existed.

Patterson died in 1972, swearing the footage was real. Gimlin mostly stayed quiet until 2005 and then started doing the Bigfoot conference circuit. Neither got rich. If it was a hoax, it was the worst get-rich scheme ever.

But here's what matters for our story: the film became a Rorschach test. Scientists saw anatomy. Skeptics saw a guy in a suit. Believers saw vindication. Everyone saw exactly what they expected to see.

In 2022, the Travel Channel's *Expedition Bigfoot* team laser-scanned the site and overlaid it with the original footage, calculating Patty's height at around 6'3". Tall, but not impossibly tall. Just ambiguous enough to keep the debate alive forever.

Sound familiar? Replace "Bigfoot" with "celebrity scandal" or "political leak." Same dynamic. The footage is grainy enough that you can't prove it's fake, yet clear enough that you can't dismiss it entirely. Everyone fills in the gaps with their own biases.

The Patterson-Gimlin film proved that evidence doesn't resolve debates; it amplifies them. Give people ambiguous visual proof, and they'll see their beliefs reflected back. The technology to do the analysis has gotten better, but the fundamental problem remains: when you want to believe badly enough, every shadow becomes proof.

The Dawn of Digital (1980s–2000s): The Democratization Begins

In 1981, Quantel released the Paintbox, a computer system that cost $250,000, more than most suburban houses. It looked like a refrigerator mated with a spaceship console, humming with the heat of its processors, demanding its own air-conditioned room. Television producers would gather around it like priests at an altar, watching in reverence as operators (called "Paintbox artists") manipulated reality with a stylus that cost more than a car.

The Paintbox could do in seconds what used to take hours in a darkroom. Color correction? Instant. Remove that telephone pole ruining the shot? Gone. Make the politician's skin look healthier for the evening news? Done before the commercial break. NBC bought one. Then CBS. Then ABC. Within two years, no major television production was untouched by digital hands.

The business world barely noticed. CEOs were still dictating memos to secretaries, filing cabinets were still made of metal, and "computer" meant that beige box in accounting. They should have been terrified.

By 1989, the warning shot was fired, although nobody recognized it as such. *TV Guide*, America's most-read magazine, with 16 million weekly subscribers, put Oprah Winfrey's head on Ann-Margaret's body for its cover. The composite was flawless. Oprah's warm smile perfectly matched Ann-Margaret's sultry pose in a gauzy dress that Oprah had never worn, would never wear. Millions of readers had no idea until an industry newsletter exposed it weeks later.

The magazine's defense was breathtaking in its casualness: it needed Oprah for the cover story about television personalities, but it wanted a more "glamorous" body. *TV Guide* saw nothing wrong with this. The controversy lasted exactly one news cycle. Within six months, *National Geographic* (the gold standard of photographic integrity) would move pyramids closer together to fit its vertical cover format. If the magazine that documented reality for a century could shuffle the pyramids like furniture, what did "real" even mean anymore?

Then came February 1990. Two brothers from Michigan, Thomas and John Knoll, released Adobe Photoshop 1.0 for $895. Thomas was a doctoral student studying image processing; John was a visual effects supervisor at Industrial Light & Magic. They'd created it to solve their own problems. Thomas needed to display grayscale images on his black-and-white monitor, and John needed better tools for the films he was working on. They thought maybe they'd sell a few hundred copies to photography enthusiasts.

The Knoll brothers had no idea they'd just democratized deception.

Suddenly, anyone with a Macintosh Plus had the same power that once required a quarter-million-dollar Paintbox and a trained operator. The teenager in the basement could do what network television couldn't have afforded five years earlier. Every business headshot became suspect. Was that hairline real or cloned? Every product photo raised questions. Was that shine natural or painted? Every marketing material entered an arms race of perfection that continues to this day.

I saw this transformation firsthand in my VFX work. When I started in 2005, Photoshop had already been entrenched for 15 years. The shame was gone. Clients didn't ask sheepishly anymore; they demanded. "Make me look 10 years younger." "Remove 20 pounds." "Fix my jawline." "Can you make the product look more premium?" "The CEO wants his hair fuller."

By 2010, the requests had become surgical in their precision. I remember one session with a Fortune 500 executive who spent three hours directing me on his headshot. "Lower the hairline. . . no, too much. . . raise it a pixel. . . smooth that wrinkle but leave the ones that make me look distinguished. . . make my eyes 5% larger. . . actually 3%. . ." When we finished, he looked at the screen and said, without irony, "Perfect. This is exactly how I look."

The iPhone had just introduced front-facing cameras in 2010, and Instagram was born that same year. Suddenly everyone was their own photographer, their own editor, their own brand. By 2015, when I was deep in commercial VFX, clients weren't just asking for perfection; they were asking for impossibility. Products that defied physics. Skin that looked human but had no pores. Reality that was better than reality.

We were training an entire generation to expect reality to be negotiable. Every Instagram filter, every Snapchat lens, every beauty app was teaching people that their actual face was just raw footage, waiting to be edited. By the time I started experimenting with deep-fakes in 2019, the groundwork had been laid. People were already comfortable with synthetic versions of themselves. The only difference was who controlled the editing.

The 1994 film *Forrest Gump* turned this private manipulation into public spectacle. Robert Zemeckis spent $65 million to seamlessly insert Tom Hanks into history. There he was, shaking hands with JFK, standing beside John Lennon, teaching Elvis to dance. The technical achievement earned an Oscar for Visual Effects, but the cultural impact was far more profound.

Audiences didn't just accept these impossible interactions; they celebrated them. Film critics called it "magical realism." Historians worried about "the pollution of the historical record." But ticket buyers? They made it the highest-grossing film of 1994. We had collectively agreed that visual evidence had lost its monopoly on truth, and we were entertained by the deception.

Ken Ralston, the VFX supervisor, later admitted his own unease: "We were very aware that we were treading on sacred ground. These were real people, real moments. We could make Kennedy say anything, make him do anything. The only thing stopping us was taste."

By 1999, *The Matrix* stopped pretending and asked the question directly: "What is real?" The film's digital effects were revolutionary (bullet time, the green rain of code, the rippling mirrors of reality), but its philosophical challenge cut deeper. In a world where anything could be digitally created, simulated, or altered, how could anyone be certain of anything?

The Wachowskis were documenting a cultural anxiety that was spreading like a virus. Y2K loomed. The dot-com bubble stretched toward its breaking point. Digital technology was rewriting every assumption about commerce, communication, and reality itself. Morpheus offering Neo the red pill was a metaphor for a choice we were all facing: accept the comfortable lie of edited reality, or confront the uncomfortable truth that we could no longer trust our own eyes.

The internet age turned this philosophical question into a practical crisis. Chain emails exploded across the newly connected world, each one carrying shocking photographs that felt too incredible to be fake, too terrible to ignore. The tourist standing atop the World Trade Center as the plane approached (shared millions of times before anyone noticed he was wearing a winter coat in September). The shark leaping from the ocean to attack a military helicopter (forwarded by your aunt, your coworker, your mother-in-law, all of whom "couldn't believe it!").

Politicians discovered the power of manufactured evidence. The 2004 U.S. election saw John Kerry's service record questioned, with photos that were later proven to be manipulated. By the time the truth emerged, the damage was done. Truth limped behind fiction, a dance that would become the defining characteristic of the deepfake era. Fact-checkers were always playing catch-up to fiction-spreaders.

By 2004, "photoshopped" had evolved from a brand name to a verb to an accusation to a universal defense. Every unflattering image could be dismissed as "obviously photoshopped." Every incriminating photo could be defended the same way. The word became a get-out-of-jail-free card for anyone caught in a compromising position. Truth had become partisan, evidence had become optional, and certainty had dissolved.

The business world catastrophically missed what was happening. Executives fixated on doctored headshots, oblivious to AI labs teaching machines to generate reality from scratch. Meanwhile, in computer science labs around the world, AI researchers were teaching machines to generate reality from scratch. The era of moving pixels was ending. The era of creating them from nothing had begun.

The Deep Learning Revolution (2000s–2017): When Machines Learned to See

In 2012, at the ImageNet Large Scale Visual Recognition Challenge (the Olympics of computer vision), something seismic happened. For years, the competition had seen incremental improvements, teams shaving off percentage points of error. Then a team from the University of Toronto, led by Geoffrey Hinton, submitted an entry called AlexNet that didn't just win; it obliterated the competition.

The previous year's winner had a 26% error rate. AlexNet achieved 15.3%. In the world of machine learning, that gap was like watching a high school track team suddenly run a four-minute mile. The secret was deep learning: neural networks with multiple layers that could learn hierarchical patterns, building understanding from simple edges to complex objects, mimicking the way the human visual cortex processes information.

The victory sent shockwaves through Silicon Valley. Google immediately hired Hinton and his team for an undisclosed sum rumored to be in the tens of millions. Facebook poached Yann LeCun from NYU. Microsoft grabbed anyone with neural network experience. The AI winter that had frozen research funding for decades thawed overnight. Suddenly, computers were learning to see, understand, and, eventually, create.

The breakthrough moment for synthetic media came on June 10, 2014, at Les 3 Brasseurs bar in Montreal. Ian Goodfellow, a PhD student under Yoshua Bengio, was arguing with fellow researchers about a seemingly impossible problem: could a neural network generate new data rather than just classify existing data? His colleagues were pitching complex statistical methods involving Boltzmann machines and intricate mathematical frameworks. The ideas were theoretically sound but computationally nightmarish.

Goodfellow had a different idea. After several beers and heated debate, he went home to his apartment on Rue Saint-Urbain, opened his laptop, and started coding at 11 p.m. By 5 a.m., he had the first working prototype of what he called a generative adversarial network, otherwise known as a GAN.

The concept was breathtakingly elegant: two neural networks locked in an eternal duel. The generator creates forgeries, and the discriminator spots them. Each failure makes both stronger, like a master forger facing off against the world's best art authenticator, each pushing the other toward perfection. The generator learns to create increasingly convincing fakes. The discriminator learns to spot increasingly subtle flaws. The end result: synthetic data indistinguishable from reality.

Within six months, GANs were generating faces. Although the initial results were ghostly, warped things that looked like they'd melted in the sun, they were faces that had never existed, conjured from pure mathematics. The implications were staggering, and by 2015, the faces were getting better.

The academic world exploded with variants: DCGANs, StyleGANs, CycleGANs. Each paper pushed the boundary further. NVIDIA's research team, led by Tero Karras, began producing faces so realistic that distinguishing them from photographs became impossible. The training process that once took months now took weeks. What took weeks would soon take days.

By 2016, the race to manipulate reality in real time had begun. A joint team from Stanford, Max Planck Institute for Informatics, and University of Erlangen-Nuremberg unveiled Face2Face at CVPR 2016. The demonstration was chilling in its casualness. Matthias Nießner,

49

Very Brief History of Synthetic Media

one of the lead researchers, sat in front of a webcam making expressions: smiling, frowning, moving his mouth. On the screen next to him, George W. Bush, Vladimir Putin, and Donald Trump mirrored his every movement in real time.

The technology required an RGB-D camera ($600 worth of equipment) and a decent graphics card. That was it. No production studio. No render farm. Just consumer hardware turning world leaders into digital puppets. The YouTube demo got millions of views. The comments section was a mix of amazement and existential dread. "We're doomed," wrote one commenter. They weren't entirely wrong.

That same year, at the Adobe MAX conference in San Diego, November 2016, Adobe's principal scientist Zeyu Jin stepped on stage for what seemed like a routine product demo. "We all know Photoshop," he said. "Today, I want to show you VoCo: Photoshop for voice."

The auditorium was packed with designers, developers, and journalists. Jin played a 20-minute recording of his colleague speaking and then typed a completely new sentence on his laptop. When he hit Enter, the colleague's voice spoke the new words perfectly. Same tone, same cadence, same subtle accent. Words the colleague had never said, would never say, now existed as audio indistinguishable from reality.

The crowd's reaction was visceral. Some gasped. Some laughed nervously. During the Q&A, comedian Jordan Peele, who was in attendance, asked the question everyone was thinking: "Can we make Trump say whatever we want?" The room went silent. Jin's response was diplomatic, but everyone knew the answer was yes.

Adobe never released VoCo publicly. In internal meetings, Legal raised concerns about liability. Marketing worried about brand damage. Engineering argued for responsible disclosure. The project was shelved indefinitely. But the genie was out of the bottle. Within months, independent researchers had replicated the technology. Lyrebird, Descript, and Resemble AI all launched commercial voice-cloning services.

Then, in December 2017, the dam burst.

A Reddit user with the handle "deepfakes" (their real identity remains unknown) posted to the subreddit r/deepfakes with a simple title: "I made my own celebrity porn." The post included links to videos where Gal Gadot's face had been mapped onto an adult film actress's body. The technology used was FakeApp, built on TensorFlow, Google's open-source machine learning framework.

The crucial detail: this ran on consumer graphics cards. Again, not supercomputers, and no specialized hardware required. The same GPU used for playing *Call of Duty* could now swap faces in a video. The user included tutorials, sample code, and step-by-step instructions. Within 24 hours, the subreddit had 15,000 subscribers. Within two weeks, 100,000.

The content being created was vile: nonconsensual pornography targeting actresses, musicians, and private individuals. But the technology itself was neutral, and it was spreading faster than anyone could contain it. Discord servers sprouted, and Telegram channels shared datasets. GitHub repositories forked exponentially.

On February 7, 2018, Reddit banned r/deepfakes. Pornhub, Twitter, and Discord followed with their own bans. But enforcement was impossible. The code was already on millions of computers. Tutorials existed in dozens of languages. The knowledge couldn't be unlearned.

What Hollywood had spent millions perfecting for *Rogue One*'s CGI Princess Leia could now be approximated by a teenager with a gaming laptop and a weekend to spare. The tools of deception had been completely made mainstream. And I was right there, watching it unfold from my desk in Los Angeles, knowing this was the technology I'd been waiting for my entire career. The convergence of everything I'd learned in VFX with the unlimited potential of AI. I had to be part of it.

The Viral Era (2018–2023): When Business Met Deception

April 2018. BuzzFeed released a PSA that changed everything. Barack Obama appeared onscreen, warning about deepfakes. Halfway through, the image split, revealing comedian Jordan Peele as the puppeteer. "We're entering an era in which our enemies can make anyone say anything," Obama's image warned.

The video went viral faster than most genuine presidential addresses. A deepfake warning about deepfakes. Fiction serving truth. The paradox was perfect.

This was the landscape when I created my Cardi B/Will Smith mashup in 2019. Under the moniker Myster Giraffe, I produced something that exploded across social media, garnering millions of views in days. The reactions told me everything: this technology had crossed a threshold. People knew it was fake and loved it anyway. But that same week, I watched similar technology used for darker purposes.

By the end of 2019, deepfake pornography accounted for 96% of deepfake videos online. Women comprised 99% of targets. Apps like DeepNude could "undress" photographs in seconds. The same tools that created joy were destroying lives.

Politics became a battlefield. A slowed-down video of Nancy Pelosi, making her appear drunk, was shared millions of times on Facebook. It wasn't even sophisticated, just simple speed manipulation, but it demonstrated how eager people were to believe what confirmed their biases. Facebook refused to remove it, setting a precedent that would haunt the next several years.

But here's what changed everything for business: the money.

In 2019, criminals used AI voice cloning to impersonate a CEO's voice, instructing an employee to transfer €220,000. By 2021, similar attacks were happening weekly. A bank in the UAE lost $35 million to voice-cloning fraudsters. The FBI issued warnings, but defenses lagged behind attacks.

I saw this coming. During my Sinatra experiment, when I fooled a deepfake detection company in its own job interview, I proved how unprepared businesses were. If I could do it as an experiment, what could criminals do with real motivation?

The Tom Cruise deepfakes on TikTok in 2021 showed the next evolution. Created by Chris Ume, these weren't obviously fake. They were perfect. Millions of followers couldn't tell the difference. The message was clear: if one person could become Tom Cruise, what was the value of identity itself?

By 2022, "deepfake" entered common vocabulary. Surveys showed that 70% of people had heard of deepfakes, but fewer than 30% were confident they could spot one. The "liar's dividend" emerged, and anyone caught in compromising footage could claim it was a deepfake. Reality had become negotiable.

The Industrial Era (2023–Current): The New Normal

In early 2023, something shifted. Deepfakes stopped being a novelty and became infrastructure. The release of tools like Stable Diffusion, Midjourney, and DALL-E 2 in 2022 had democratized image generation. By 2023, video was following suit. ElevenLabs could clone anyone's voice with three minutes of audio. By early 2024, that requirement dropped to under a minute for some services. D-ID and Synthesia could create professional spokesperson videos from text. HeyGen could translate videos into any language with perfect lip-sync. A single photograph could become a talking head; a brief voice recording could generate extended speech.

Then, January 2024 brought the Taylor Swift incident. Explicit AI-generated images spread across social media, accumulating tens of millions of views before platforms could respond effectively. X (formerly Twitter) temporarily blocked searches for Swift's name. The White House press secretary addressed the issue. Swift's team pursued both legal action and platform accountability, contributing to industry-wide policy changes. Meta began rolling out synthetic content labels. TikTok introduced AI disclosure requirements for realistic content. YouTube mandated that creators mark AI-altered videos in certain categories.

The entertainment industry, after years of resistance, began adapting to the inevitable. Digital doubles entered film contract negotiations. James Earl Jones signed an agreement allowing his voice to be used for future Darth Vader appearances through AI technology. The 2023 Hollywood strikes brought AI and digital replicas to the forefront, with SAG-AFTRA securing provisions about consent and compensation for digital doubles. Background actors remained particularly vulnerable, with some contracts allowing perpetual use of their digital likenesses for minimal compensation.

Virtual influencers gained serious commercial traction. Lil Miquela, operating since 2016, expanded her brand partnerships into the millions. Aitana López, Spain's AI influencer, created in 2023, reportedly generates substantial monthly income through brand deals and subscriptions. Companies launched their own virtual ambassadors. The distinction between human and synthetic influencers grew increasingly irrelevant to engagement metrics.

The 2024 global election cycle saw widespread adoption of AI-generated content. In India's general election, political parties used AI to create multilingual content, with candidates appearing to speak languages they hadn't recorded in. Indonesia's election featured

AI-generated content showing candidates appealing to younger voters. In Pakistan, Imran Khan's PTI party used AI to create speeches while he was imprisoned. Mexico, Turkey, and dozens of other nations saw similar deployments. The United States experienced its own wave, including robocalls using cloned voices and manipulated video content.

Corporate adoption accelerated rapidly. Zoom introduced AI Companion features that could summarize meetings and draft responses. Microsoft Teams added avatars for video calls. Customer service departments deployed increasingly sophisticated AI agents. Some banking customers interacted with AI representatives without realizing it. Real estate platforms offered virtual tours with AI guides speaking multiple languages. Mental health apps deployed AI counselors, raising both accessibility benefits and ethical concerns about the nature of therapeutic relationships.

Technical barriers continued falling. Runway's Act-One could transfer acting performances to CG characters. Meta's Emu Video could generate short clips from text prompts. ByteDance released tools for facial animation from single images. These capabilities moved from research labs to consumer applications. Mobile apps offered face-swapping and voice cloning to anyone with a smartphone.

Legal systems worldwide struggled to respond effectively. The European Union's AI Act, which began implementation in 2024, included provisions for synthetic content labeling. China introduced requirements for deepfake content marking and registration. U.S. states passed various laws addressing nonconsensual intimate images and deepfake fraud, creating a patchwork of regulations. Federal legislation remained stalled. Enforcement proved challenging across all jurisdictions.

The detection and authentication industry expanded rapidly. Companies like Reality Defender, Sentinel, and others raised significant funding to provide enterprise deepfake detection. Intel's FakeCatcher claimed high accuracy rates in controlled conditions. TrueMedia.org launched free detection tools for journalists and fact-checkers. Yet detection remained an arms race, with each advancement in detection met by improvements in generation.

Financial institutions discovered that their voice biometric systems were vulnerable to synthetic voice attacks. Insurance companies began offering deepfake-related coverage while excluding it from standard cyber policies. Courts grappled with evidentiary standards for video and audio evidence. The "deepfake defense" emerged in criminal proceedings, with defendants challenging the authenticity of digital evidence.

Cultural adaptations emerged organically. Families developed code words after scammers used voice cloning in fake emergency calls. "Send me a selfie" became a common verification request. Dating apps introduced various forms of verification badges. Professional contexts saw a return to in-person meetings for sensitive discussions. Notaries and law firms adapted their practices to address authentication concerns.

By late 2024, synthetic media tools were embedded everywhere. Every major video conferencing platform offered some form of AI enhancement or avatar option. Social media platforms integrated AI generation tools directly into their creation interfaces. Adobe's Firefly allowed complex video editing through text prompts. Google and OpenAI competed to release increasingly capable video generation models.

The normalization was evident in everyday use cases. Corporate executives used AI avatars for routine meetings. Educational content featured synthetic presenters. Dead performers appeared in new productions through estate agreements. Political candidates delivered simultaneous speeches in multiple locations via AI doubles. Students submitted video presentations that they technically never recorded.

As I write this in 2025, the evolution continues. OpenAI's Sora creates impressive videos from text descriptions. Anthropic, Google, Meta, and others race to release competing capabilities. New startups emerge weekly with specialized applications. The tools that required significant technical knowledge just two years ago now run in web browsers.

Looking ahead to the next year or two, the trajectory suggests even more accessible and capable tools. Real-time interactive deepfakes, persistent digital personas, and seamless integration into everyday communication platforms all appear technically feasible. The infrastructure adapts daily. Corporations build workflows around synthetic media. Governments establish task forces and departments. Educational systems teach media literacy with new urgency.

Conclusion: The Eternal Return

So here we are, 150 years after William Mumler's spirit photographs, carrying in our pockets more powerful manipulation tools than entire Hollywood studios possessed just a generation ago. The technology has transformed beyond recognition, but the human elements remain remarkably consistent.

We still want to believe comforting lies. We still use images to rewrite history. We still struggle to distinguish truth from fiction, and, perhaps more troublingly, we're not always sure we want to. The same psychological vulnerabilities that made Victorian audiences believe in photographed ghosts make modern audiences share deepfaked politicians.

But there's a crucial difference between then and now. Those spirit photographs fooled thousands; today's deepfakes can deceive billions instantly. Mumler's trial was a local sensation; today's synthetic media scandals are global crises. The stakes have escalated from individual fraud to societal epistemology. We're now questioning the nature of evidence itself.

History's lesson is clear: every generation develops new tools for deception, then slowly, painfully develops the wisdom to live with them. Photography forced us to question images. Photoshop forced us to assume manipulation. Deepfakes are forcing us to reimagine how to interact with a source of unknown origins.

Yet humans adapt. We learned to live with photography despite spirit photos. We learned to navigate television despite propaganda. We learned to use the internet despite misinformation. We will learn to live with deepfakes, too, not by preventing them (that ship has sailed) but by developing new frameworks for trust and verification and, perhaps most importantly, new acceptance that our eyes and ears may not be reliable.

The tools that began as weapons of deception have also become instruments of creativity, education, and connection. The same technology that can fake a CEO's voice can also let a stroke victim speak again. The same systems that create nonconsensual pornography can also let historians bring ancient figures to life for students. The same algorithms that undermine political truth can also democratize filmmaking, letting anyone become a director.

This is the duality we must navigate: every tool powerful enough to enhance human capability is also powerful enough to exploit human vulnerability. The question isn't whether synthetic media is good or bad; it simply is. Like fire, like writing, like the internet, it's a technology that fundamentally changes how we interact with reality and each other.

As you continue reading this book, as you learn to protect yourself and your business from the malicious uses of deepfakes, remember this history. Remember that we've been here before, in different forms, with different technologies but the same human challenges. Remember that the solution historically has never been to stop the technology but to evolve with it.

The ghosts that William Mumler photographed in 1872 weren't real, but the grief of the people who bought them was. The deepfakes flooding our feeds in 2025 aren't real either, but their impacts (financial, political, personal) absolutely are. Understanding this distinction, navigating this gap between the synthetic and the significant, that's the challenge of our time.

You asked how we got here. The answer is: the same way we always have. One innovation, one deception, one adaptation at a time. The difference now is the speed, the scale, and the stakes. But the path forward remains the same, too: awareness, education, and the remarkably human ability to adapt to whatever reality (real or synthetic) we find ourselves in.

Welcome to the age of synthetic media. Your eyes may deceive you, but armed with knowledge and history, your judgment doesn't have to.

What's Next?

From Mumler's ghostly photographs to Stalin's vanishing commissars, from Photoshop's democratization to the Reddit user who gave deepfakes their name, each generation's tools for manipulating reality have followed the same arc. Innovation, exploitation, normalization. The technology changes, but human nature doesn't. Understanding this history reveals that we've always been susceptible to visual deception, but knowing this doesn't automatically protect us from it.

This is where the story gets personal. While the world was still treating deepfakes as a technological curiosity, I was already living in that future as Myster Giraffe, wielding this technology, testing its limits, discovering both its incredible creative potential and its terrifying capacity for harm. The tools that could resurrect DMX for one final performance could just as easily destroy someone's reputation with a fabricated scandal.

In the next chapter, we'll explore this double-edged nature not through theory but through real experiences: the exhilarating moments when this technology enhanced human connection, and the sobering realizations of how easily it could sever that same connection.

Chapter 3

The Double-Edged Sword: Illuminating the Duality

There's no light without shadow and no shadow without light. Every bright idea casts its own darkness, whether we notice it or not. Deepfake technology is no different. It's like a beam of sunlight streaming into a room, revealing beautiful details we never thought possible, while casting long, unshakable shadows that creep into corners we can't always see.

Light and shadow exist together, locked in an eternal dance. You can't pull them apart, no matter how hard you try. It's this duality that defines deepfakes. On one hand, they hold the power to inspire, to create, to elevate, and to unlock stories we couldn't tell before. On the other hand, they carry a quiet, almost insidious danger, the ability to deceive, disrupt, and undermine trust in ways we're only just beginning to understand.

When I started experimenting with deepfakes, I was captivated by the light. Who wouldn't be? Here was a tool that felt like magic, something that could transform raw data into a seamless piece of art, a living, breathing moment that had never existed before. It was exhilarating. For someone like me, steeped in the world of visual effects, it felt like stepping into a whole new dimension of creativity.

But as the light grew brighter, the shadows grew longer. I began to see how this same technology could be twisted into something darker. A voice manipulated to steal millions. A face swapped to spread disinformation. A trusted medium turned into a weapon.

The very same tools that had given me so much joy could just as easily be used to sow chaos.

It was a sobering realization, like standing in a room where the sun is so bright that it blinds you to the darkness creeping at the edges. You can't ignore it once you've seen it. That's what this chapter is about: looking at both sides of deepfakes. Not just the bright, hopeful side where creativity and innovation thrive, but also the shadowed corners where trust is eroded and truth becomes a casualty.

The good and bad aspects of deepfakes, like light and shadow, are inseparable. They exist in a delicate balance, each shaping and defining the other. To understand one, you have to confront the other. That's why I've come to see my role as less of a creator and more of a dimmer switch. Every project is an opportunity to dial the brightness up or down. Some days I'm illuminating possibilities. Other days, I'm keeping the glare from blinding us. Control isn't about intensity. It's about balance.

The Promise of Light

Deepfakes are a spark—a bright, dazzling light that has the power to transform industries, inspire innovation, and upend the way stories move through time. When I began working with this technology, I was struck by how limitless it felt. What once took massive infrastructure, teams of specialists, high-end equipment, and studio signoff could now emerge from a laptop and a determined mind. You didn't need permission anymore. You just needed vision.

Imagine this: a teacher in a middle-school classroom conjures up an interactive, lifelike version of Abraham Lincoln to explain the Gettysburg Address. Not just reading it or teaching it, but walking students through the "why" of the Gettysburg Address, in real time. Or a filmmaker brings a long-lost actor back to life to complete a performance that stalled out decades ago, preserving a final work that no one expected to see finished. No longer are these ideas figments of science fiction. They're increasingly becoming the domain of weekend creators and independent storytellers. New tools of the AI era are bridging the gap between thought and action.

In my own work, I saw this potential come alive. The Cardi B and Will Smith mashup wasn't just funny, it was a stress test. It showed that deepfakes could remix culture in ways even the culture wasn't ready for. It felt like kicking down a door that no one had noticed was locked. That video forced people to reckon with a new kind of visual fluency. Some called it hilarious. Others called it unsettling. Both were right. And that tension? That's where the magic lives.

With Myster Giraffe, I've had a front-row seat to what happens when creativity and synthetic media collide. One of the most profound projects I worked on was bringing DMX back to life. The iconic rapper passed away on April 9, 2021, at the age of 50. Years after his passing, I was approached to create a deepfake that allowed him to perform a song he had recorded but never released: a track he had finished over a decade earlier. The result wasn't just a curiosity. It felt like a broadcast from another timeline (see Figure 3.1).

Figure 3.1 Digital resurrection brings DMX back to perform an unreleased track
Source: Generated with AI usingCustom AI Software – AIMultiple

The Double-Edged Sword: Illuminating the Duality

Experience the emotional power of ethical deepfakes.

The project was primarily about pulling off the trick of presence. Could we make the world feel like DMX was back? Could we re-create the magic that was DMX? Fans watched that video and didn't say, "What a great fake." They said, "Man, I miss him." That distinction is incredibly important. It meant we'd crossed a line, not of deception, but of emotional continuity and connection. It's easy to forget how hungry people are to feel something real, even when it's built with pixels and code.

This is the unexpected power of deepfakes: not manipulation, but emotional recovery. The ability to revisit a voice. Reframe a moment. Reanimate something unfinished. Not all memories are complete, and many times, you don't want the truth back; you just want the person. And this technology, if used carefully and, more importantly, ethically, can crack open that door. None of this is accidental. The same tools that produce cheap gags can, in the right hands, become instruments of grace. But the cost of that grace is intention. It has to mean something; otherwise it's just noise.

So yes, the spark still dazzles. But I don't chase it the same way anymore. This work transcends novelty and technical showmanship. The focus has shifted to responsibility and purpose. The work gets brighter. The shadows get longer. And if you're not careful, the tool starts leading the hand. These days, I keep asking myself the same

Behind the AI Mask

question: "What will this moment *mean* for the people who see it?" If I can answer that honestly, then maybe I still deserve to hold the match.

I remember the first time I got paid for a deepfake job like it was yesterday. It was for a Halsey music video. Halsey is an R&B pop star from America, known for her haunting melodies and striking visuals. I was well seasoned in visual effects, so taking money for deepfakes felt like an extension of what I already did. It was just another tool to accomplish a vision and to make magic on a tighter budget. Back then, deepfake was still new and still a curiosity, but I treated it like any other VFX job.

That project with Halsey and Kelsea Ballerini was my first taste, but it was just a warmup. A few months later, I got called in to fix a Budweiser campaign featuring Halsey, called "Be a King." She was telling her story, from sleeping in subway stations to her meteoric rise to fame. The Budweiser team had hired a much larger multinational studio, but Halsey wasn't happy with the results they produced. She felt it wasn't good enough and that it didn't represent her correctly.

Enter stage right: Myster Giraffe, called in to fix the work that never saw the light of day because of the unintentional misrepresentation of someone's likeness. Because I wasn't present during the initial shoot, when they shot the footage, the lighting in those subway scenes was a mess. Now, this being a new technique, it was very mysterious to most people, including industry veterans. I can't completely blame them. Here I was, stepping in as an unknown guy with the ability to correct their missteps. I could feel the judgment dripping through on the Zoom calls where Budweiser connected me with the post-production facility so we could work out where there was room for improvement. To say there was prejudgment and criticism would be an understatement.

To pull this off, I had to collect publicly available data from Halsey wherever I could find it: a little interview data here, a little finesse there. At this stage, I was well equipped from my time spent with the

Super Deepfake Squad, and I had designed the absolutely perfect way to collect custom data from a subject with my work at Aliza.

In the end, I completed six shots over nine days. It paid handsomely, and more than that, it further cemented in my mind that I was wielding something powerful. Yes, it takes technical skills to achieve this level of quality with such limited resources, but it was also about having a secret sauce no one else could replicate. Deepfakes had become my superpower. The realization shifted my entire perspective. This technology could revolutionize how people connect, how brands communicate, and how stories reach audiences.

From the very beginning, Myster Giraffe was more than just a creative project. It was a social science experiment, a living study of how people connect with culture, caricature, and how humor bridges the gaps. Every single post I made was a calculated move. I wasn't just creating to entertain myself; I was meticulously mapping out what would resonate with an audience and how far I could push that resonance before it snapped.

I developed an instinct for what would be reposted and what wouldn't, and I never needed to ask my audience directly. I could feel it. It was a bizarre sensation that generally came as an internal tickle. My heart would do a bit of a dance in my body, and my spine would tingle with anticipation of the way it feels to go viral. It became a very familiar feeling—so familiar, in fact, I knew when I had a hit on my hands the same way Quincy Jones must've felt when he was working on Michael Jackson's *Thriller* album. The trick was making sure the audience was always in on the joke. That's why my work never felt like a cheap shot. I wanted people to laugh, to share, and to feel like they were part of something amazing, never that they were the punchline.

Myster Giraffe's work had become so prolific and honorary, I had celebs and pop stars reaching out to see if I could create a custom deepfake video for them. Ray J., Trevor Noah, Anderson Paak, and more.

That's the response you get when you're aiming for inclusion and joy, ensuring that everyone can take a second and laugh a bit.

As I navigated the technical challenges of creating these videos, I also became more attuned to what the world was feeling. The pandemic had reduced everyone's lives to a series of endless news alerts and rising death counts, but there was still room, maybe even a desperate need, for humor. Every video was a test of timing and tone, of how to bring just a few seconds of relief to timelines otherwise filled with grim updates. I saw how these quick bursts of levity resonated with people—how even a short, funny clip could break through the tension. The more I shared, the more I understood that the real power of deepfakes was never truly in the technology, but in how they made people feel, good or bad.

It was a process that got refined with every post. If something didn't hit, I would watch the comments and tweak my approach, but never compromise the core of what I was trying to say. Over time, that instinct became one of my biggest strengths. It's what separated me from everyone else trying to do the same thing. For me, deepfakes had become telling the right story at the right time, and I had learned exactly how to do that.

Restoring What Was Lost

There's another layer I haven't yet been able to realize, and one I still hope to. I've always dreamed of using deepfakes to help people who may not have access to this kind of technology, people who could use it to reclaim something deeply personal. One of the ideas that has stuck with me is offering burn survivors the ability to see themselves as they were before their injuries. Not to erase who they are now, but to let them reconnect with who they were. A kind of emotional restoration that modern medicine can't provide, but digital tools might.

I reached out to national burn centers. I reached out to individual influencers who had gone through major fire-related transformations. I was ready to donate the time, the effort, the energy. But no one took me up on it. Maybe it was too soon. Maybe the idea itself was too uncomfortable. Still, that instinct never left me.

Even though no one took me up on it, the idea kept pulling at me. It didn't fade away when the emails and DMs went unanswered. It grew, reshaping itself in my mind until it grew past the burns of influencers and victims of unfortunate circumstances. It transformed into the possibility of connection itself.

There's a motto I think about often: remember the human. That's the compass. That's the power. We can keep making things for clicks, for laughs, for noise. Or we can remember why we create in the first place. We can help people hold onto the people they never got enough time with. That's the real magic, not just showing the past, but letting people *feel* it again, even if only for a few fleeting moments. And that magic has to be handled with care. I've always believed that kindness is free. That idea has become the foundation for everything I do with deepfakes, and it's become a guiding principle about the choices I make as a creator.

I'll agree that it's easy to get caught up in the technical wizardry, to treat it all like a game of one-upping the next guy, but we should be careful with this technology.

> There's a motto I think about often: remember the human.

People would always come to me with ideas, things they thought I should be doing with this technology. They wanted me to sell products with deepfakes. They wanted me to package it up, turn it into a tool, license it to everyone. There was so much money on the table, but I never wanted to pursue any of the opportunities presented to me. My vision was always to create a content series, to build something that was bigger than just a cool trick or a quick payday. If I couldn't do it the way I wanted to, then I didn't want to do it at all.

That's the lesson that has carried me through every decision since. It doesn't matter how tempting the opportunity is. If it doesn't line up with the story I'm trying to tell, with the kind of creator I want to be, I'll walk away. Because for me, success comes from trusting my own voice and maintaining creative integrity, beyond financial rewards or publicity. That foundation remains unshakeable—no external force can compromise what you've built from within.

The Ones We Know

I think about what it could mean to let someone talk to a version of their mother or father who passed, to hear a loved one's voice say their name one more time. I think about what it would feel like to ask your grandfather about the war again, or to let your kids hear bedtime stories told by someone they never got to meet. These moments don't belong to Hollywood. They don't need budgets or trailers or premieres. They're private. Intimate. Sacred.

And yet there's a strange tenderness in thinking about doing this with people in my own life. The idea of digitally preserving someone I love—my grandmother, my uncle, even my own mother—feels at once hopeful and slightly intrusive. It's one thing to offer the gift of presence to someone else. It's another thing to ask for it.

How do you bring that up? How do you say, "Would you mind if I capture your voice, your expressions, your laugh, just in case I need to hear them again one day?" It feels fragile. Delicate. Too close to grief, even if grief hasn't arrived yet. There's something sacred about letting people go. About healing without needing to replicate. And yet . . . there's also something deeply human about wanting or even needing to *remember with precision*.

Technology gives us that possibility. Not to replace someone. But to experience them in a new dimension. I haven't asked my aging relatives to let me preserve them. But I know that someday, I probably will. And when that day comes, it won't be about freezing them in time. It will be about giving time back to them. To us.

The tech isn't quite there. The world isn't quite ready. But it's coming. And when it does, we'll need to ask hard questions. Who owns that likeness? Who has the right to restore it? Who decides when it should be retired? This will be a new kind of ethical terrain, one that doesn't look like privacy law or copyright, but more like stewardship.

We built this technology to feel more human. So let's use it that way.

The Torajan Reminder

In some ways, bringing back the dead in this way is not a new idea. The Toraja people of Indonesia have been doing something like this for generations. In their culture, the dead aren't gone in the way most of us think. They are still part of the household, part of the rhythm of life. They're spoken to. Fed. Dressed. Honored. Their presence doesn't vanish with death; it just changes form.

To the Torajans, a loved one who has passed is not dead. They are "to macula" or sick. The body remains in the home for months, even years, while the family continues to care for them. Meals are delivered. Conversations are had. Children grow up knowing their grandparents as more than photos in frames. Eventually, an elaborate funeral marks the person's transition to the next world, but that connection, that sense of companionship, never really ends.

I think about that when I imagine the future of deepfakes used for remembrance. This technology serves continuity rather than mere illusion. We fear resurrection when it feels like denial. But what if it's devotion? What if remembering someone vividly is a form of cultural respect, a way of saying, "We carry you with us, always"?

In Western culture, we often fear clinging too long to the past and are told that eventually it's time to move on. But what if holding space for those who shaped us is what helps shape the people we become? What if honoring our ancestors visually, vocally, and/or digitally isn't creepy or indulgent, but necessary?

If we do not respect those who came before us, we risk losing respect for what we're building now. The Torajans remind us that legacy is not something buried. It's something nurtured. Deepfake technology can do the same, if we choose to build it with reverence, and in our pursuit of remembering others, we must recognize our own future place in the chain of memory.

What They'll Say with My Voice

There's a saying that goes, "Every person dies twice. Once when they stop breathing, and a second time when someone says their name for the last time." That used to be a poetic truth. Now, in the age of cloud storage, AI models, and digital trails, we have to question whether that second death is even possible anymore. The Internet doesn't forget. And if we choose to feed it enough of ourselves—our faces, our voices, our rants, our fears, our laughter—it will remember us longer than we remember ourselves.

If someone collected all of your emails, texts, social posts, audio logs, and private thoughts recorded in any corner of the cloud, would they be able to reconstruct you? Would they get a convincing version of who you were? I think they might. Not perfect, but meaningful. Because we're not made from perfection. We're made from patterns. We're not defined by the things we all share. We're shaped by the tiny, weird details: the stories we tell again and again, the way we say our favorite words, the people we trust to see our most unfiltered thoughts.

And that's what a good model learns. Not just the obvious stuff. The edges. The glitches. The history is baked into repetition. If you train it well enough, and if you feed it with love and context and nuance, it stops sounding like an impersonation and starts sounding like *you*.

That's the challenge and the opportunity. A data model is only as good as the soul it's trained to carry. If we do this right, the digital versions of ourselves might not just be echoes. They might be companions. Teachers. Anchors. Not synthetic ghosts, but extensions of memory.

But do it wrong? And all you're left with is a hallucination in your own voice. So the question becomes: what are we training the future to remember? Are we training it to remember the truth of us, or just the performance? The nuance, or the highlights? Are we leaving behind the curated version of ourselves, or the honest one? Because if all we pass down are the things that went viral, the things that looked best through filters and framing, we may be building legacies from veneers, not values.

The ground truth isn't in the polish. It's in the contradictions. The hesitation in a voice note. The second-guessing in a DM. The way someone tells a story differently depending on who's in the room. Those are the things that make us who we are, and those are the details that are hardest to capture in code.

And yet, if we get this right, we don't just preserve the past—we inform the future. We offer our descendants not a perfected monument, but a working map of how we tried, failed, adapted, and carried love forward. We leave behind not just image and audio, but *intention*. And maybe, just maybe, that's enough to keep the light on a little longer.

The Shadow of Deception

Every light casts a shadow. And the brighter the potential of deepfakes became, the harder it is to ignore their darker side. For all the doors this technology can open, it can just as easily be used to slam others shut.

Take the example of businesses targeted by deepfake fraud. I've read stories of companies where a CEO's voice was convincingly mimicked, tricking employees into authorizing six-figure wire transfers. They're real incidents, and although I haven't spoken personally to the victims, the implications are chilling: the erosion of trust in our most basic communication. Imagine trying to run a company where you can no longer trust a phone call, a video meeting, or even a recorded statement.

Beyond financial loss, these attacks fundamentally shatter institutional trust. And once trust is broken, it's almost impossible to repair.

And it doesn't stop there. Deepfakes have been used to spread disinformation, altering videos to make public figures say things they never said. In one high-profile case, a manipulated video of a politician went viral just days before an election, casting doubt on their integrity and shifting public opinion. By the time the video was debunked, the damage was done.

> That's the shadow side of deepfakes: a world where nothing can be taken at face value, where even the most trusted sources can be weaponized against us.

The most unsettling part? You don't always see it coming. The biggest damage doesn't always come from something you post. It comes from what someone else does with it. This is the *black swan problem,* described as a rare, improbable event that often has disruptive effects that stem from unexpected information that comes to light. The term "black swan" originates from the historical belief that all swans were white. The discovery of black swans in Australia challenged this long-held assumption, demonstrating the possibility of events existing outside of long-held knowledge.

A single clip, taken out of context, twisted by bad actors, and fed through the outrage machine, can do irreversible damage in hours.

The Double-Edged Sword: Illuminating the Duality

You don't get a heads-up when something goes off the rails. You just wake up and realize you lit the match.

Then there's the personal toll. I've read stories of people whose lives were upended by malicious deepfakes. Fake videos that ruined careers, damaged relationships, and in some cases, drove people to despair. The shadows don't just lurk. They move fast.

The Balancing Act

Standing between light and shadow isn't easy. It's not just about understanding the potential of deepfakes. It's about recognizing the responsibility that comes with them. As a creator, every project feels like walking a tightrope. On one side, there's the pull of innovation and creativity. On the other hand, there's the weight of consequences.

Early on, I asked myself the hardest question a creator can ask: Should I? Not can I. Not how fast can I get it out. Should I?

When I created my first viral deepfake, the Cardi B and Will Smith mashup, it was pure fun. People loved it, shared it, laughed with it. But as the numbers climbed, I started feeling that pressure I now recognize so well. What if it had gone the other way? What if someone ripped it from context? What if it fueled disinformation or spun into something cruel or dehumanizing?

It wasn't enough to just be good at creating. I needed to be accountable. So, much like I established a code of ethics to guide how Myster Giraffe creates content, I built a framework I now call *Ethical AI Stewardship,* which serves as a survival tool. My rules were simple but strict:

- Always respect the subject's humanity and dignity.
- Make sure the joke includes the subject, not targets them.
- Stay within parody and legality, never stepping into exploitation.

Although this is designed to avoid blowback, it's also about earning trust. Because once people believe you're capable of anything, they have to believe you won't use that power against them.

No one celebrates what you didn't release. No one shares the clip that never saw daylight. But that silence? That's the work. It's not showy, and it won't trend. But it keeps the world from catching fire. Ethical restraint doesn't make headlines, but it builds something more valuable: long-term trust. That's leadership most people will never see.

Just Because You Can

I remember a fellow creator from the Super Deepfake Squad, one of the sharpest technical minds in the space. They made a deepfake that depicted Volodymyr Zelenskyy violently beating Vladimir Putin with a baseball bat, composited into a scene from *Inglourious Basterds*. It was graphic, visceral, and politically loaded. And although it was undoubtedly a technical marvel, I couldn't stop thinking: *Is this where we're headed?*

The creator called it protest art. And maybe it was. Maybe it was a way of channeling anger, outrage, grief, everything that swirls around war and injustice, into something people would share. But for me, it crossed a line. Not because I disagreed with the sentiment, but because I know what happens when content like that leaves its creator's hands. Context gets lost. Nuance gets burned away by virality. And suddenly, a protest becomes a provocation. A catharsis becomes a weapon.

I stay away from politics in my work, and that's by design. Not because I'm afraid to have an opinion, but because I know that political content amplifies every risk—from immediate backlash to chronic misinterpretation. You risk pouring gasoline on a fire you can't control. And in this space, where people already don't know what's real, I don't want to add to the noise. I don't want someone using my work to validate a point I never meant to make.

75

The temptation to shock, to provoke, to go viral, it's real. But so is the cost. And in the age of deepfakes, that cost might not be yours to pay. It might land on someone else entirely.

When the Joke Lands Too Well

Sometimes, the danger isn't in something being misinterpreted. It's in it being *perfectly* interpreted, and still misunderstood. That's a reality I learned firsthand.

There was a time I put Tiffany Haddish's face on Prince during a deepfake performance. It was clean. Seamless. Technically, it was one of my best early outputs. But something strange happened. People didn't get the joke: not because it wasn't funny, but because it looked too real. The comments poured in, not questioning the authenticity, but treating it as if it *were* authentic. "Tiffany's so talented," they'd say. Or, "Girl, I hope that's a wig. I hope you didn't cut your hair."

In those moments, the deepfake wasn't treated like a remix; it was treated like a receipt. It passed every unconscious test viewers use to decide what's real, and in doing so, it *broke* the intent. No one stopped to think, "Wait, is this even possible?" They just accepted it. And that acceptance, although flattering on a technical level, was a gut punch on an ethical one. If people didn't know it was fake, then had I misled them? Even if it wasn't malicious, had I still disrupted their sense of reality?

That wasn't the only time my work took on a life I hadn't planned. I've seen blog pages, clickbait outlets, and even high-traffic but low-tier online news sites use my work as visual bait, embedding it in hot takes or polarizing posts just to stir up conflict in the comments. They weren't interested in the art. They were interested in what the art could *do* for them: spark outrage, bait shares, and drive traffic.

If I had known the paths some of these clips would take, I might not have released them. That's the burden of this medium. You can control your intent, but once it's out there, you no longer own the context. The Internet takes it. It strips it, bends it, captions it, reposts it, and uses it for its own ends. Sometimes that's harmless. Sometimes it's not. And unless there's public outrage, no one's calling the original creator. They're just moving on to the next thing.

Those moments reinforced something I've come to accept: the better your work gets, the more dangerous it becomes *if* it's misunderstood. When a deepfake is obviously fake, it invites curiosity. But when it's too good, it can become invisible. That's when people stop questioning and start believing. And that, to me, is a sign that your own success demands even more responsibility, not less.

The Power of Saying No

One of the hardest lessons I've learned in this space is the power of saying no. It's not easy to turn down a project, especially when it's creative, lucrative, or high-profile. But there are moments when you have to look at an idea and think: this crosses a line.

I remember one project that came from a client in New Zealand. It was for a Boys and Girls Club-type organization, and the concept was undeniably clever. They wanted to use deepfakes of powerful, yet negatively viewed, world leaders as children. The message was simple: if these figures had received more love, time, and consideration in their youth, maybe they wouldn't have grown up to be such harmful people.

On the surface, it seemed like a poignant and thought-provoking campaign. But the more I thought about it, the more it didn't sit right with me.

The deeper I thought, the more it felt like I was watching a train roll toward a cliff in slow motion. It had all the makings of something that could be brilliant, but also all the ingredients for a PR nightmare. It wasn't just a question of legality. It was the kind of thing that felt like it would look fine until it was out in the wild. Until someone spun it, clipped it, or framed it with the wrong headline. And by then? Game over.

These were real people, real identities, being used for a paid campaign without their consent. Even if the message was ultimately positive, I would have been misrepresenting them. And misrepresentation, when paired with paid work and international exposure, is where I draw the line.

For me, there's a big difference between creating something for parody or fun and getting paid to use someone's likeness in a way that could harm or mislead. Parody brings people into the joke. It lets them laugh with you, not at you. But when you step into the realm of commercial work, where the stakes are higher and the reach is global, you have to take a step back and decide where your boundaries are. For this project, I knew I couldn't cross that line.

Saying no wasn't easy. The concept was strong, and the execution would have been a creative challenge I'd have loved to tackle. But it was the right decision. Because if I can't trust my own instincts, if I can't hold to my own principles, then how can I expect anyone else to trust me?

Shadow Can't Exist Without Light

Light and shadow are inseparable. The brighter the light, the deeper the shadow. This duality demands understanding rather than fear.

Deepfakes aren't inherently good or bad. They're tools, shaped entirely by the intent and integrity of the people who use them.

For me, this realization has been both humbling and empowering. It's humbling because it forces me to confront the responsibility I carry as a creator. Every project, every decision, has the potential to tip the balance toward light or shadow. But it's also empowering because it reminds me that I have a choice. I can decide how to use this technology. I can decide which projects to take on, which risks are worth it, and where to draw the line.

This responsibility extends beyond individual creators to encompass our entire society: creators, businesses, policymakers, and everyday people, standing at the intersection of light and shadow, deciding how to shape the future. The tools are here. The technology is advancing. The question isn't whether deepfakes will continue to grow. It's whether we'll guide them responsibly or let them spiral out of control.

Standing between light and shadow isn't always comfortable. It requires hard conversations, tough decisions, and a willingness to say no, even when it's inconvenient. But it's also where the most important work happens. It's where we build trust, where we set boundaries, and where we create a foundation for something better.

The real power doesn't come from turning everything all the way up. It comes from knowing how to tune it. Knowing when to brighten and when to soften. That's the responsibility we carry. Not just to create, but to calibrate, because not everyone will calibrate. Not everyone wants balance. For some, the shadow becomes an invitation rather than a warning. That's the part we don't like to admit. Although the innovation empowers the curious, it also arms the reckless.

So what happens when people use this power not to illuminate, but to obscure? Not to bring stories to life, but to bury the truth beneath convincing lies? That's where we're headed next.

Because for every uplifting project, every legacy deepfake crafted with care, there's another version of this story playing out in the dark. And if we're going to talk about the promise of light, we have to confront the weight of its opposite. Welcome to the dark side of innovation.

But before we fully step into that darkness, there's one more story worth telling because it captures the moment when the power of the tool outpaced the wisdom behind it.

Another creator I once worked alongside in the Super Deepfake Squad decided to use *Sesame Street* as a canvas. The idea was

The Double-Edged Sword: Illuminating the Duality

technically clever. He took scenes from the show and overlaid deep-faked faces, then bleeped out Elmo's words in a way that made it sound like he was swearing. It was outrageous and absurd, and it got laughs in private circles. But it also crossed an invisible line.

Sesame Street holds foundational status in American media. It's one of the few places in the cultural landscape that still holds trust between parents, children, and the stories they grow up with. That trust is fragile. Messing with it, even as a joke, risks confusing the most impressionable audiences—and that's when the problem transcends taste to become a matter of ownership. Three of those deepfakes were flagged almost immediately by the rights holders. A YouTube channel with almost 300,000 subscribers received three strikes in less than 24 hours. And just like that, it was gone.

Years of work, wiped in an instant. Not because the tech failed, but because the instinct to entertain outpaced the instinct to reflect.

That's what happens when we stop calibrating. When we test boundaries for fun and forget that some of those boundaries were drawn for a reason. Not to limit creativity, but to protect the people it might reach.

What's Next?

What follows is a closer look at how that trust forms in the first place. Why we believe what we see and hear. Why some moments slip past our defenses without us even noticing. The next chapter explores the psychology of belief and how deepfakes tap into the very instincts that help us make sense of the world.

Chapter 4

The Dark Side of Innovation

Trust is one of humanity's most powerful yet fragile constructs. It is the invisible thread that holds our relationships, societies, and institutions together. But trust isn't built on logic alone. It is deeply wired into our psychology, and that is exactly why deepfakes are so dangerous.

Beyond manipulating pixels, deepfakes manipulate perception. They hijack the cognitive shortcuts our brains rely on to decide what is real. They turn our own instincts against us. To understand how, we have to start with why we trust images, video, and sound in the first place.

For most of human history, survival depended on our ability to quickly assess reality. When our ancestors saw a lion, they didn't pause to consider the philosophical implications of its existence — they ran. Our brains evolved to process sensory information rapidly and efficiently, prioritizing speed over perfect accuracy.

This is where *cognitive heuristics,* mental shortcuts, come into play. Instead of analyzing every detail of a situation, we make snap judgments based on patterns we recognize. These heuristics are incredibly useful in everyday life. They help us navigate conversations, read facial expressions, and distinguish reality from deception.

One example is the *availability heuristic,* a mental shortcut where people judge the likelihood of an event based on how easily they can recall similar instances. For example, plane crashes are extremely rare, but because they receive widespread media coverage, people tend to overestimate their frequency. The vivid imagery of plane wreckage and the disaster area leaves a lasting impression, making air travel seem more dangerous than it is.

But here's the problem: deepfakes exploit these very shortcuts, hacking our perception in ways our brains weren't designed to defend against.

The Trust Bias: Why We Believe What We See and Hear

Our trust in images and video has deep biological foundations. Psychologists call this the *truth bias:* the innate tendency to believe that the information presented to us is real unless we have a reason to suspect otherwise. This bias is so strong that even when people are told they're looking at a fake image, many still react to it as if it's real.

Think about the last time you saw a news report with a video clip. Did you question its authenticity? Probably not. We're conditioned to accept visual and auditory evidence as the ultimate proof of reality.

Photographs don't lie, right? This belief was ingrained in society for over a century before Adobe Photoshop came along. Video is even more trustworthy. If something moves and speaks, it must be real. Live audio? Almost unshakable. A phone call from a familiar voice is one of the most convincing forms of communication.

Deepfakes weaponize this trust bias by fabricating visual and auditory evidence that seems indistinguishable from reality. And because our brains are wired to accept this evidence, we struggle to resist the deception, even when we know deepfakes exist.

Although the historical reliance on visual media explains why people trust what they see, the deeper mechanism lies in human psychology. Trust is hardwired into our biology, an evolutionary shortcut that helped early humans survive. If you saw a predator or danger, trust in your visual and auditory senses meant the difference between life and death. Over millennia, this instinctive trust extended beyond immediate survival, becoming integral to interpersonal relationships and societal structures.

However, this deeply ingrained trust is not infallible; it is highly susceptible to manipulation. One of the key psychological vulnerabilities deepfakes exploit is *confirmation bias*. This cognitive shortcut causes people to accept information that aligns with their preexisting beliefs while dismissing information that contradicts them. In the context of deepfakes, confirmation bias amplifies their potency.

For instance, if a person dislikes a public figure and sees a deepfake of that individual making offensive remarks, they are more likely to believe it, regardless of its authenticity. The deepfake doesn't have to be flawless; it only needs to align with their worldview. Confirmation bias creates a shortcut for belief, bypassing critical thinking and skepticism.

This vulnerability is compounded by emotional manipulation, another psychological tool deepfakes wield with precision. Humans are emotional beings, and content that provokes outrage, fear, or validation tends to bypass rational scrutiny. Studies have shown that when people are emotionally aroused, their ability to analyze information critically diminishes. Deepfakes weaponize this phenomenon by crafting narratives that evoke strong emotional responses, whether through shock value, humor, or fear.

Take, for example, a deepfake video depicting a politician in a compromising situation. Even if the video is later debunked, the emotional reaction it provokes, outrage or distrust, lingers in the public consciousness. This makes deepfakes particularly dangerous in environments like social media, where content spreads rapidly and emotional engagement drives virality.

The Perception Hack: How Deepfakes Trick Our Brains

To understand how deepfakes manipulate people, we need to break down the specific ways they exploit our cognitive vulnerabilities. The following sections do just that.

The Face Trust Heuristic

Our brains are specialized to recognize and interpret faces. The *fusiform gyrus,* a region of the brain dedicated to facial recognition, allows us to detect even the subtlest facial movements and emotional cues. Deepfakes mimic these cues with remarkable accuracy, making them feel "real" even when they aren't.

The Voice Familiarity Effect

We recognize people by their voices almost as reliably as by their faces. Research shows that hearing a familiar voice triggers emotional and cognitive responses associated with that person.

Deepfake audio exploits this by almost perfectly replicating tone, cadence, and inflection, making it nearly impossible to distinguish from a real conversation.

The Fluency Effect

The easier something is to process, the more likely we are to believe it. This is why clear, high-quality video or audio seems more credible than distorted or low-resolution content. Deepfakes are getting sharper, cleaner, and more seamless, fooling not just the untrained eye but even experts.

The Emotion Trap

When a video triggers a strong emotional reaction, whether it's outrage, fear, or admiration, we become less likely to scrutinize it critically. Deepfake scams and disinformation campaigns rely on this, crafting content designed to provoke immediate emotional responses that override logical analysis.

The Experiment: How Easily Can We Be Fooled?

The psychological research painted a clear picture, but I wanted proof. Having spent months studying how our brains process trust and visual information, I was ready to test these vulnerabilities firsthand in real-world interactions.

So, I utilized an AI-powered mask that allowed me to transform my face in real time. No prerecorded footage. No post-production. Just a live, interactive deepfake. Then, I went where people least expected to be fooled: one-on-one video calls with complete strangers.

If deepfakes were as powerful as I suspected, I wouldn't need high-tech cyberwarfare tactics. I wouldn't need elaborate planning. I wouldn't even need to be convincing. All I had to do was show up and see if people questioned what they saw.

I set up my AI mask based on a popular but currently unfamiliar person from history, and then I turned on the camera.

Omegle connects you to a random person from anywhere in the world with just a click. No filters, no pretense, just two strangers face to face. And in call after call, people simply accepted what they saw. It wasn't just that they believed the deepfake; it was that they didn't even think to question it. They looked at me, talked to me, and responded naturally, completely unaware that the face on the screen was AI-generated. For the first time, I saw real-time deepfake deception in action, not just in theory.

The Politeness Barrier: Why People Refuse to Question Reality

I expected people to call me out. I expected them to ask questions, to hesitate, to look closer. But they didn't. It wasn't disbelief that struck me the most; it was silence. Out of hundreds of video calls and random connections, only one person outright asked if my face was real.

One.

At first, I thought it was just because people ignored their instincts. That was part of it. When something feels slightly off but not blatantly wrong, people tend to override their initial gut reaction. But as the experiment continued, I realized something even more unsettling: once you make it past that initial hurdle of doubt, the deception isn't just accepted. It becomes the new reality.

It wasn't just that people ignored their initial instincts and moved on. It was that once they decided I was real, they committed to that reality. From that point on, everything I said, every expression I made, was processed as genuine. They didn't question me because they didn't want to. No one wanted to be rude. No one wanted to point out something that might be embarrassing or awkward. It's the same social reflex that keeps us from asking a stranger if they're pregnant unless we're absolutely sure. But more than that, once their brain took the shortcut and accepted what was in front of them, there was no turning back.

Yet again, I had another realization that deepfake deception centers on bypassing that single hesitation point, not merely tricking the eye. Beyond stopping their questions, they fully embraced the illusion.

The Wildest Real-Life Failures of Deepfake Detection

The idea that deepfakes are a future problem is a lie. They're already here, already fooling millions, and already exposing how unprepared we are. Some of the biggest failures in detection have already played out in real time, with real-world consequences.

Joe Says No

A fake Joe Biden robocall in January 2024 hit voters in New Hampshire, using AI-generated audio to impersonate his voice and tell people not to vote in the upcoming primary. The call falsely claimed that voting in the primary wasn't necessary and that waiting until November's general election would be the correct course of action. The message was entirely fabricated, but that didn't stop it from spreading before fact-checkers could catch up. By the time officials became aware of the deception, it had already reached thousands of voters. The damage was done before the truth had a chance.

Investigators traced the origin of the robocall to political consultant Steve Kramer, who admitted to commissioning the deepfake recording. Kramer claimed that he wanted to highlight the dangers of AI in politics, but his method—paying $500 for a synthetic voice

Hear the AI-generated voice that attempted to suppress voter participation.

model and distributing the call through a telemarketing firm—crossed ethical and legal lines. The Federal Communications Commission (FCC) responded by proposing a $6 million fine against Kramer, and Lingo Telecom, the company that transmitted the robocalls, agreed to a $1 million settlement. The incident made clear that deepfake misinformation is no longer a hypothetical risk; it's an active weapon being deployed in elections.

X Marks the Spot

Social media platform X (formerly Twitter), in one of its many chaotic policy shifts, handed out verification badges to AI-generated influencers, treating them as legitimate accounts before quietly revoking their status. The fact that artificial faces could pass as real ones wasn't just an oversight. It was a sign of how easy it is for deepfakes to blend into the background of digital life.

The debacle raised serious concerns about the effectiveness of Twitter's verification process. The AI-generated influencers, designed to resemble real people, amassed thousands of followers before the company took action. Many users had engaged with these accounts, believing they were real individuals, and some had even formed online relationships or business connections with them. The situation exposed a critical flaw in the platform's ability to detect AI-generated identities and raised alarms about the potential for similar incidents in more sensitive contexts.

By the time X acknowledged the mistake, the damage was already done. Users who had interacted with the fake influencers were left questioning their own ability to discern reality from fabrication. The lack of transparency in how and why these accounts were initially verified only deepened distrust in the platform's policies. It wasn't just about one verification mistake; it was about the realization that AI-generated personalities could seamlessly integrate into the digital ecosystem, potentially influencing discussions, spreading misinformation, and even altering public opinion.

Celebrity Connections

Then there are the scammers. A group of con artists successfully used deepfake technology to create fake celebrity video shoutouts, tricking people into believing their favorite stars had recorded personal messages. The resemblance was close enough to fool fans, and because deepfake video detection tools are still unreliable, platforms had little ability to stop the fraud.

What made these scams even more insidious was how they exploited the trust fans placed in their favorite celebrities. Many of the fake shoutouts were tailored for personal occasions: birthday messages, congratulatory notes, and even charity endorsements. Victims not only lost money but also experienced a sense of betrayal upon realizing the truth. Some of these deepfake videos were used in promotional material for fraudulent events, leading to ticket sales for fake meet-and-greets or appearances that were never going to happen.

Platforms attempted to crack down, but the sheer number of these videos made it difficult to police them effectively. Fraudsters continually adapted, using new techniques to make their fakes even more convincing. As a result, some celebrities began issuing public warnings about deepfake impersonations, urging fans to verify video endorsements through official channels. However, with AI-generated content becoming more sophisticated, even seasoned professionals found it difficult to distinguish authentic messages from manipulated ones.

Fake Endorsements

Some cases of deepfake scams evolved beyond celebrity impersonation. Businesses found themselves dealing with fake video endorsements from industry leaders, crafted to look like executives personally vouched for a product or service. Customers, convinced by the credibility of these artificial endorsements, invested in scams that left them with nothing. This shift from targeting individuals to manipulating corporate reputations highlighted how deepfake deception threatens personal identity theft, financial fraud, and large-scale consumer manipulation.

Even government agencies and security firms are struggling to keep up. Law enforcement has begun encountering cases where criminals use deepfake technology to impersonate executives in corporate fraud schemes. A CEO appearing on a video call, seemingly issuing financial directives, can turn out to be an AI-generated deception orchestrated by scammers. Some banks have already reported multimillion-dollar losses due to deepfake-driven scams.

Deepfake Pornography

Meanwhile, deepfake pornography continues to thrive, often targeting women and public figures. Detection methods exist, but they are ineffective against the sheer volume of fake content generated daily. Victims are left with few legal options, as laws struggle to catch up to the speed of AI manipulation.

The psychological and emotional toll on victims is devastating. Many women have spoken out about the harassment, shame, and reputational damage that follows when their likeness is used in explicit content they never consented to. The Internet's permanence makes removing these videos nearly impossible, as copies proliferate across different platforms faster than takedown requests can be processed. For many victims, the damage to personal and professional lives is irreversible.

Attempts to curb the spread of deepfake pornography through legislation have been slow and inconsistent. Although some jurisdictions have enacted laws targeting nonconsensual deepfake content, enforcement remains a challenge. Many perpetrators operate anonymously or outside the reach of domestic legal systems, making prosecution nearly impossible. Additionally, social media platforms and content-hosting sites have been criticized for their lax response, often failing to remove harmful content swiftly enough to protect victims.

Some advocacy groups have pushed for stronger regulations and better technological solutions, such as AI-driven detection tools that flag manipulated content before it spreads. However, the sophistication of deepfake technology means that detection methods are often one step behind. Without widespread cooperation from governments and tech companies, the problem is likely to escalate, leaving more victims in its wake.

The Trust Shortcut: Why Deepfakes Work in Social Settings

Even more powerful than the visual illusion is the *trust transfer* effect. In some cases, I had friends introduce me to someone they knew—a spouse, a coworker, a sibling. I'd ask them to introduce me as a friend or colleague, and I'd pretend to be interested in whatever I passively knew about them, like their job, a hobby, or their new car purchase. Because they trusted the person making the introduction, they automatically extended that trust to me. This blew my mind. It meant I didn't even need to be convincing. If I was introduced by someone they trusted, the deepfake was instantly accepted without question. Think about what that means.

If a scammer impersonates a CEO, their voice doesn't have to be perfect. If a deepfake politician gives a speech, it doesn't have to be flawless. The illusion only needs to be good enough for the brain to take a shortcut. Once the brain fills in the gaps, the deepfake isn't just believed, it becomes reality.

The experiment didn't end when the conversations ended. When I finally turned off the AI mask and revealed my real face, the reactions were intense. Some people laughed, some were stunned, and some immediately disconnected the call. One reaction stuck with me.

A guy I had been talking to for nearly 10 minutes stared at me and said, "I don't get it. So . . . who was I just talking to?" His confusion confirmed what the experiment had proven: deepfakes rewrite reality in real time, doing far more than simply fooling people. And if I, a single person experimenting with AI, could do this to random strangers . . . what happens when bad actors weaponize this technology?

When Curiosity Looks Like a Con

The deeper I went into real-time experimentation, the more unsettling the reactions became, not because people were disturbed by what they saw, but because they weren't. Friends didn't recognize me. Strangers believed every pixel. And more than once, I had someone send me one of my own deepfake videos, unaware that I was the person behind Myster Giraffe.

But the wildest reactions came on Omegle.

After enough sessions using the AI mask in real time, the platform began flagging my IP. The users weren't reporting me for harassment or violence. They were flagging me because they felt tricked. That feeling of being certain you knew what you were looking at, only to find out you didn't, was enough to make people uncomfortable. For some, it crossed a line.

I get that. In their minds, I was no different than a scammer. But in mine, I was running a live field study. I wasn't harvesting data or stealing identities. I was trying to answer a question: *Where are we, as a society, in our ability to tell real from fake?* What's the current calibration of trust, and how easy is it to bypass?

I approached it like a scientist would approach a lab rat. Only this time, the lab was the Internet, and the rats were human behavior patterns. The data I collected wasn't numbers like a traditional scientific trial; it was the looks on people's faces. It was their silence. It was how quickly they fell into the illusion, and how violently they reacted when it broke.

I would normally start with a standard conversational opening: "Hey, how are you doing today?" You know, like a normal person would. I would then ask them if they felt something was out of the ordinary with my video feed. "Do you see anything out of the ordinary with what you're seeing? Something about what you're seeing right now isn't real. I want to see if you can guess the culprit." Situated behind me was a plant, a bookshelf, a wall, and so on. The unwitting subject would take a moment and normally respond with no, primarily because they trust their eyes 100 percent, and nothing immediately triggered their internal system of verification. The ones who chose to give an answer other than "no" would guess something besides my face. After a couple of moments of tension and "What's this guy on about?" energy, I'd turn off my AI face, and most would either react with horror and immediately click to leave or respond with genuine curiosity.

When Omegle flagged my IP address, I was disappointed. But what struck me was that my disappointment didn't come from being banned. It came from how effective the deception was. I expected skepticism. I got trust. I expected confusion. I got belief. The fact that it was so easy, and that even the people closest to me couldn't spot the difference, made it clear that on a global scale, we weren't ready. Not even close.

The reason I chose Omegle was that it offered the most diverse set of data: a worldwide connection to any user from any interconnected country on the planet. I connected with people from the United States, the UK, Australia, New Zealand, France, Spain, India, and more. The behavior I received from the overall study participants didn't vary from country to country. Everyone reacted the same. Every country. I even connected with some college students in the UK who were studying machine learning. Even they, who are in every sense ahead of the curve versus their local population, were fooled.

And that's when it hit me. If everyone around the world reacted like this to *me*, someone with absolutely no malicious intent, how would they respond to someone trying to do real harm?

The Emotional Cost of Doubt

I've never had someone look me in the eye and say, "I don't know what's real anymore." But I've felt it myself. Plenty of times.

There are moments—quiet, frustrating moments—where I'm watching something online, and I just don't know. Not for sure. And that's coming from someone who lives in this world, someone who's in the 99th percentile when it comes to recognizing deepfakes, AI artifacts, and the invisible fingerprints synthetic media leaves behind.

Most of the time, you can see it if you know where to look. There's a certain texture to it, a rhythm that doesn't quite feel organic. The glitches aren't always visual. Sometimes they're behavioral. A pause that shouldn't be there. A facial tick that doesn't match the personality. Audio that dips ever so slightly out of sync, or a cadence that feels pulled from a different context.

The funny thing about social media now is that I see these things from morning until night. Deepfakes are absolutely everywhere. It's wild how easy it's become to generate something that looks believable. A few taps. One prompt. That's all it takes now. The results are often crude, lazy, and unrefined, but it's better than the alternative: being manipulated in real time and not even knowing it.

And that's what scares me most. I know there are people out there, people with my level of skill or better, who have far fewer scruples.

If the rough stuff is already slipping by unnoticed, what happens when the good stuff hits? What happens when the content is indistinguishable, not just to the average person, but to someone like me?

Short form is where it gets really dangerous. The clips are fast. The context is missing. Your brain fills in the gaps before your gut has time to object. And by the time you start to feel something is off, you've already shared it. You've already reacted. You've already been manipulated.

I mentioned earlier that time is the enemy of a scam, and this is why. Given enough time, humans are excellent at spotting deception. Our brains are natural scam detectors; however, we don't walk around with them on all the time because it's exhausting. We want to believe because it's easier that way.

But the future we're hurtling toward will force us to leave those detectors running. Not out of paranoia. Out of necessity. We'll start second-guessing glints in people's eyes. The way someone laughs. Whether a wink was really a wink or a composite glitch stitched from training data. It's going to mess with the social contract we've taken for granted our whole lives. When you can't trust your eyes, society doesn't just get blurry. It comes undone.

We now exist at a crossroads, one where any piece of footage can be reasonably questioned, not just by skeptics but by the people caught in it. If someone doesn't like how they appear in a video, they can say, "That's fake," and in many cases, they won't be wrong. That's the terrifying new baseline.

Think about the implications. A video surfaces. It looks damning. But it's been compressed, re-uploaded, clipped, and filtered through half a dozen platforms. Its fidelity is shot. So what do we do? We call in a digital forensics expert to examine what's left of the original. They make their best approximation, but it's still an approximation. At that point, truth becomes a matter of interpretation.

This isn't a hypothetical. This is the playbook now. In a world where even truth is negotiable, real events can be dismissed with a shrug and a soundbite. We've already seen the rhetoric: "It's AI." "That's not me." "This has been manipulated." It doesn't even need to be true. The mere *possibility* is enough to stall accountability and fracture public opinion.

This is a disaster scenario in the making. A viral video capable of triggering civil unrest, or worse, potentially a civil war, could be waved away with a well-timed denial. The information cycle moves too fast and too furiously for the public to catch up. By the time the forensic report drops, the damage is already done.

Platforms share the burden of triage, of scrubbing falsehoods before they metastasize. But here's the trick: fake news isn't always obvious. What's fake to one person can be considered gospel by another. That ambiguity is a feature, not a bug. And unless we find a way to anchor ourselves to objective truth, no matter how uncomfortable, it's going to get worse.

Because without truth, we don't just lose trust. We lose the thread entirely. The world becomes unrecognizable. And in that world, no one is safe.

The Role of Big Tech in the Deepfake Crisis

For all the panic around deepfakes, the companies that could do the most to stop them aren't exactly in a rush. Social media platforms and AI developers actively profit from deepfake spread rather than passively allowing it. Every viral deepfake drives engagement, which in turn fuels ad revenue and platform growth. Tech giants have little financial incentive to take a firm stance against deepfake content, especially when their own algorithms reward provocative, emotionally charged media.

Deepfakes thrive in part because the systems that distribute them are often designed to favor engagement over accuracy, speed over verification, and profit over truth. Although some companies have attempted to address the issue with detection tools and content moderation efforts, these measures have largely fallen short against the scale of the problem.

The sheer volume and velocity of synthetic content overwhelm human moderation capabilities. The same algorithms that push clickbait articles and conspiracy theories to the top of feeds are the ones boosting deepfake content. Whether it's an AI-generated celebrity scandal, a fake CEO announcement that sends stocks into freefall, or a synthetic political speech designed to sway an election, social media companies stand to benefit from the chaos. The more people click, comment, and share, the more money these platforms make.

As someone who built Myster Giraffe, I witnessed firsthand how deepfake content spreads, sometimes far beyond my own reach. One of my deepfakes of Steve Harvey, for example, made its way across the Internet so widely that people I knew personally sent it back to me, unaware that I was the creator. It was both validating and unsettling to see how quickly and unpredictably content could travel once it was picked up by social media algorithms. Certain videos of mine escaped their "orbit" and landed in unexpected places, even making it to the celebrities I featured. I noticed how social media algorithms often prioritized engagement over context, amplifying deepfakes that sparked reactions while suppressing others without any clear reasoning.

Identifying the Boundaries

Before we even talk about Big Tech's responsibility, we have to ask a more basic question: what exactly are they flagging? Is a fake image with a fake caption enough? What about a parody clip with no disclaimer? How do we draw the line between satire and disinformation, between creative remixing and weaponized manipulation?

The truth is, we haven't drawn the line. Not clearly. And without one, it's nearly impossible to know what's getting through and what isn't. One person's joke might be another person's gospel, and that ambiguity makes it hard for platforms to step in without looking like they're choosing sides. Still, boundaries have to be drawn. Even if they're imperfect. Even if we get it wrong at first. Because without a framework, the whole thing becomes ungovernable.

Right now, I'm seeing AI-generated music paired with captions that frame it as lost material from famous artists. It's like alternate history as entertainment, but presented without any warning. There's no "what if" disclaimer. The content appears as established fact. This content rewrites culture in real time while misleading audiences. And once that kind of revisionism takes hold, it's hard to undo.

Imagine trying to research something 20 years from now, only to find the Internet littered with fake archives, synthetic photos, and AI-written fiction labeled as fact. That's not a thought experiment. It's a preview. Current moderation systems, forensic tools, and search platforms are already overwhelmed. They were built for a slower Internet, not the generative avalanche we're living through now.

Meta, for example, announced a deepfake detection tool in 2020 to great fanfare but quietly abandoned it by 2022, citing technical limitations and a lack of scalable solutions. As I mentioned earlier, Twitter (now X) verified AI-generated influencers before realizing their mistake. YouTube selectively removes deepfake content but allows others to rack up millions of views as long as they drive ad revenue. TikTok has become a breeding ground for AI-generated misinformation, and although it claims to be working on detection, the platform still prioritizes engagement.

The issue extends beyond social media. AI companies developing deepfake technology are often reluctant to impose restrictions on their tools. Open-source AI models that can create deepfakes in seconds are freely available to anyone with a decent graphics card. Some companies market these tools under the guise of creativity and accessibility, but in reality, they are handing out loaded weapons with no safety mechanisms. Ethical concerns are secondary to growth and adoption. Even when AI developers introduce disclaimers or watermarking, they are often easy to bypass or simply ignored by bad actors.

Tech companies like to position themselves as neutral platforms. In reality, they act as curators, shaping content visibility through recommendation algorithms, moderation policies, and selective enforcement. They decide which posts trend, which are suppressed, and which get buried. The failure to take meaningful action on deepfakes is not due to a lack of capability but a lack of will. The reality is that any serious crackdown on deepfakes would require a fundamental shift in how these companies operate. It would mean prioritizing truth over engagement, investing in detection tools that actually work, and, most importantly, accepting some level of responsibility for the spread of misinformation on their platforms. None of that aligns with their business model.

One proposed solution is mandatory watermarking of all AI-generated content, an idea that sounds great in theory but is riddled with problems in practice. Some regulators, such as the European Union, have begun pushing for AI watermarking standards, and companies like Google and OpenAI have experimented with embedding traceable markers in their generated media. However, the effectiveness and enforcement of these measures remain uncertain:

- Watermarking only works if every AI developer agrees to implement and enforce it.
- Even if watermarks are embedded in AI-generated content, they can be removed or altered.

- Platforms would need to check for these watermarks and act on flagged content, something they've repeatedly failed to do with existing moderation challenges.

- The burden of proof would still fall on users, businesses, and regulators rather than the companies that facilitate the spread of deepfakes in the first place.

This brings us to the larger ethical dilemma: should tech companies act as gatekeepers of truth? The idea of having corporations dictate what is real and what is fake is troubling for many reasons. History has shown that giving centralized entities the power to decide what content is legitimate can easily lead to abuse, censorship, and bias. The deepfake crisis, however, has made it clear that a completely hands-off approach isn't viable either. When anyone can create a fake video of a world leader declaring war or a CEO announcing a fabricated merger, the consequences extend far beyond social media outrage. They impact economies, elections, and global stability.

Ultimately, Big Tech isn't going to solve the deepfake crisis unless forced to through strong regulation, legal accountability, or significant financial penalties. If I had control over a platform's algorithm, I would take social media back to a chronological timeline where every follower had access to posted content. Additionally, I would require deepfake creators to label their work as AI-generated, enforcing strict penalties for repeat offenders. Ethical responsibility should not be optional, and those who ignore it should face real consequences. Policies requiring transparent AI-generated content labeling, stricter moderation enforcement, and heavy fines for platforms that fail to act against malicious deepfakes could provide the necessary push for meaningful change. The only real pressure they respond to comes in the form of regulation, public backlash, or financial risk.

Governments are beginning to wake up to the threat, with some countries introducing legislation to hold platforms accountable for the spread of AI-generated misinformation. Lawsuits and financial penalties have also started to emerge, targeting companies that allow deepfake scams and fraudulent content to thrive. As long as the financial benefits outweigh the risks, tech giants will continue dragging their feet.

Until real accountability is enforced, businesses, governments, and individuals will have to take deepfake protection into their own hands. Companies can implement internal verification policies, train employees to recognize manipulated media, and invest in AI detection tools. Individuals should adopt a more skeptical approach to digital content, verifying sources before sharing information. Governments must continue pushing for legislation that holds platforms accountable while promoting public awareness campaigns. Without proactive measures, deepfakes will only become more pervasive and difficult to counter. The platforms that claim to connect the world are fueling its growing distrust. As long as deepfakes continue to drive engagement, Big Tech has little reason to stop them.

Why Social Media Fuels Deepfakes (and Doesn't Stop Them)

If deepfakes were just a technological curiosity, they wouldn't be a crisis. But the problem isn't just that they exist, it's that they spread like wildfire. And social media platforms, the most powerful amplifiers of digital content in history, are built to accelerate the chaos.

At their core, social media companies don't care if something is real. They care if it gets engagement. Outrage, humor, and shock drive shares, comments, and watch time, all of which fuel a platform's algorithm. And deepfakes? They're engineered to be engaging.

We've seen this play out before. Every time new technology is weaponized for misinformation, platforms are slow to react. Facebook allowed political disinformation to thrive, only acting after public outcry and government scrutiny. TikTok, built on viral trends, lets AI-generated content slip through its cracks with little oversight. X verified AI-generated influencers before realizing its mistake. These aren't accidents. They're business models prioritizing reach over reality.

And then there's the ethical mess of AI-generated influencers. Digital personalities like Lil Miquela, Shudu, and countless AI-modeled brand ambassadors blur the line between what is artificial and what is authentic. At what point does the synthetic become more trusted than the real? Social media thrives on illusion, and deepfakes are the ultimate evolution of that illusion.

Deepfake videos and audio clips don't just passively exist on these platforms. They are promoted, recommended, and inserted into algorithmic feeds designed to maximize watch time. The very mechanisms that made viral videos a cultural force now work in service of synthetic media, ensuring that a compelling fake can outperform the truth. Even when platforms claim to combat misinformation, their tools often fall short. Fact-checking is slow, but deepfakes spread in seconds. Once a fake clip is embedded in people's minds, debunking it rarely undoes the damage.

Compounding this issue is the lack of a unified response from these companies. Although one platform may ban deepfakes outright, another might allow them under a creative label. Some require disclaimers, but enforcement is inconsistent at best. Without clear and universal guidelines, deepfakes continue to slip through the cracks, often surfacing where users least expect them.

The Policy Problem: The Rules Keep Changing

If deepfakes pose a clear threat to public trust and stability, it would seem logical that we'd have a coordinated system for identifying and managing them. But the reality is far more chaotic. Platforms like YouTube, TikTok, and X adjust their policies frequently, often without transparency or consistency. One month, a video might be removed for violating community guidelines. The next, similar content could be allowed with only a mild disclaimer or not flagged at all if it generates enough engagement.

Our legal systems offer little clarity, too. We haven't agreed on fundamental questions like who owns a deepfake or who is responsible for its misuse. Is it the creator who manipulates the footage, the company that provides the AI tools, or the individual whose likeness has been replicated? This absence of legal consensus has created a kind of regulatory void, where accountability is diffuse and enforcement is rare.

Technology companies have announced initiatives to address the issue, but follow-through has been inconsistent. Whether due to technical limitations or lack of incentive, meaningful enforcement remains limited. Detection is difficult, moderation is costly, and most companies continue to benefit financially from the very content they claim to regulate.

As a result, we now operate in a digital environment where misinformation travels faster than the mechanisms designed to contain it. Deepfakes flourish in part because there is no centralized authority to enforce boundaries or establish standards. Instead, we're left with a fragmented response shaped more by business interests than ethical responsibility.

This isn't simply a matter of digital policy, but more so a broader crisis of credibility. And as you'll explore in the next chapter, the consequences of this unresolved tension extend beyond online platforms. In the hands of the wrong actor, a single synthetic video can influence elections, inflame international tensions, or even serve as a pretext for war.

Understanding how we got here is only the beginning. What comes next will depend on how quickly we can define, defend, and reinforce the truth.

The Path Forward: Can We Outthink Our Own Biases?

The first step in defending against deepfake deception is understanding how and why we are vulnerable to it. Once we recognize that our brains are wired to trust images and voices, we can start implementing strategies to counteract manipulation:

- **Slow down.** If a video or audio clip elicits a strong emotional reaction, pause before believing or sharing it. It only takes a moment.

- **Look for inconsistencies.** Although deepfakes are improving, subtle flaws often remain, such as unnatural blinking, off-sync lip movements, or robotic vocal cadences.

- **Verify from multiple sources.** A single piece of evidence should never be the sole basis for belief. Cross-checking is essential.

- **Adopt technological safeguards.** AI-powered deepfake detection tools are improving, but awareness and skepticism remain the most powerful defenses.

We are entering an era where seeing is no longer believing. The question is no longer whether deepfakes will fool us, but how many times they already have. If we don't adapt now, deepfakes won't just manipulate our perception—they will rewrite reality itself.

What's Next?

This chapter walked through a landscape where perception can be engineered and instincts can be hacked. And although the threat feels futuristic, the damage is already here. Deepfakes are everywhere, and they're not just fooling us; they are exhausting us. They erode our confidence in what we see, chip away at our certainty, and create a world where even genuine moments can be doubted into oblivion.

It's tempting to respond with apathy, to say, "It's all fake anyway," and disengage. But that is the most dangerous path of all. Deepfakes do not win by being perfect. They win by making us question everything, even the truth.

We should not have to do this alone. The platforms that shape our digital world have a responsibility to slow the spread of synthetic media and support the truth instead of sidelining it. But we know better than to wait for them.

I end this chapter not with clarity, but with awareness. That is what this moment demands: quiet, constant vigilance. Because deepfakes represent both a technological threat and a test of our collective vigilance, one that tests how willing we are to pay attention when everything around us is designed to distract.

The next chapter explores what happens when deepfakes go global. When deception becomes strategy.

This moment calls for a shift, not just in how we watch, but in how we interpret. We have to retrain ourselves to engage with media more actively, not more passively. That might mean reading beyond a headline, questioning a source before we react, or simply waiting before we share. The tools we need are not all high-tech. Many of them are just habits we forgot how to use.

When manufactured reality is no longer something we scroll past, but something we vote on, fight for, or go to war over.

Chapter 5

The Rise of Deepfake Crime

A finance worker in Hong Kong joined what seemed like an ordinary video call. His company's Chief Financial Officer appeared onscreen, flanked by other senior executives, issuing instructions to transfer urgent funds. The CFO's face moved naturally. His voice carried the same calm authority it always had. The instructions were clear. The urgency was real. Trusting the process, the employee authorized the wire transfer. See Figure 5.1.

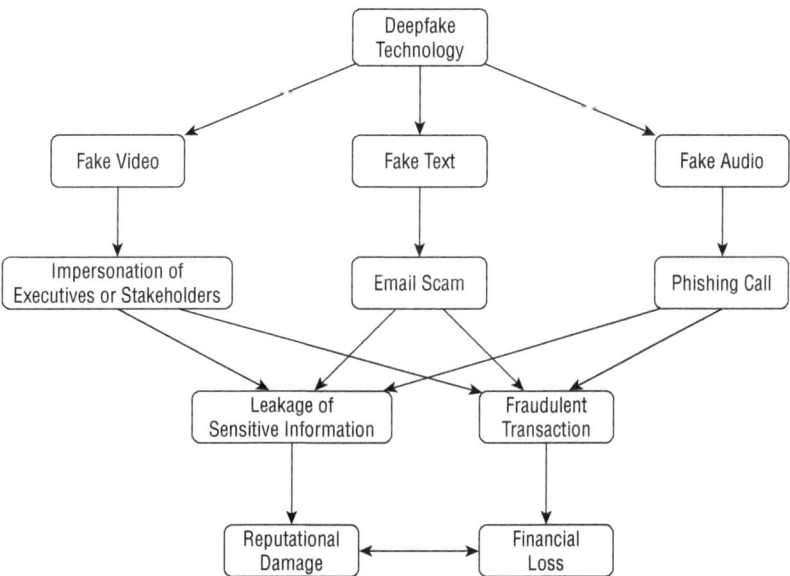

Figure 5.1 Anatomy of a $25 million deepfake heist: how criminals weaponized video conferencing trust

Source: (a) Generated with AI using Midjourney AI – Midjourney, Inc. (b) Generated with AI using Midjourney AI OpenAI

By the time anyone realized what had happened, $25 million had vanished.

The CFO and the executives had never been on the call. The entire meeting had been an illusion, orchestrated by criminals using deepfake technology to mimic the company's leadership in real time. There were no obvious glitches, no distorted audio, no mismatched lip-syncing. The deception was precise where it mattered. The finance worker wasn't fooled by a poorly written phishing email or an obviously suspicious message. He had been deceived by something far more sophisticated, an attack that felt real in every way that counted.

Deepfake scams succeed through their ability to exploit expectations rather than through perfection. The finance worker knew the CFO's face. He had heard his voice on countless other calls. Every detail was familiar enough to bypass the moment where doubt might have surfaced. Even if the deepfake was not flawless, his brain had already filled in the gaps because there was no reason to question something he had always trusted.

His morning had started like any other. He reviewed his inbox, sipped his coffee, and prepared for the scheduled call. When the CFO appeared onscreen, the finance worker barely thought twice. The lighting looked right. The background was the same office setting he was used to seeing. His colleagues nodded along, responding as they normally would. Everything about the scene was mundane, expected, ordinary. But that was what made it dangerous. There was no reason to be suspicious because nothing felt out of place.

At the end of the investigation, no arrests were made and no funds were recovered.

Trust as a Vulnerability

In hindsight, there were details in this video that might have seemed unusual—perhaps a slightly longer delay before responses, or an almost imperceptible stiffness in the executive's movements—but those microsecond hesitations never surfaced in the finance worker's conscious mind. The scam worked because it fit perfectly into the pattern of what he had come to expect. The deepfake didn't need to be flawless. It just needed to be close enough.

This scam highlights an uncomfortable truth. We are in an era where seeing and hearing no longer equate to believing. Traditional markers of authenticity, such as facial recognition, voice verification, and live video calls, are now vulnerabilities rather than safeguards. The psychological shortcuts that allow us to navigate daily interactions efficiently, the trust we place in familiar faces and voices, have become liabilities. Deepfakes exploit these instincts, allowing criminals to override skepticism with a seamless illusion of reality.

This represents a fundamental crisis in how we verify reality. For centuries, our ability to trust what we see and hear has shaped decision-making in critical areas such as business, law, and personal relationships. In courtrooms, video and audio evidence have often been regarded as irrefutable proof, determining the outcomes of high-stakes trials.

> We are in an era where seeing and hearing no longer equate to believing. Traditional markers of authenticity, such as facial recognition, voice verification, and live video calls, are now vulnerabilities rather than safeguards.

But what happens when those windows can be forged as easily as a fake signature? A video confession, once seen as the irrefutable gold standard of credibility, can now be challenged as an elaborate fabrication. A damning phone call may now become suspect, not because it lacks clarity, but because it is too perfect, too convenient, and too easy to replicate in the digital age.

Judges and juries are not forensic analysts. They rely on a bedrock assumption: that what they see and hear in evidence is an authentic record of the truth. Deepfakes absolutely break that assumption. They turn every piece of evidence into a potential trick, every voice into a mask. In this new environment, prosecutors find themselves forced to defend not just the narrative of a case, but the very reality of the evidence that supports it. Defense attorneys, in turn, gain a powerful new tactic: the ability to sow doubt not by proving an alibi, but simply by raising the possibility of a digital forgery.

This shift not only changes the rules of the courtroom but also reshapes the stakes. For centuries, justice has depended on the idea that you can test the credibility of a witness: that you can trust the camera, the tape recorder, the archived voicemail. Deepfakes collapse that distinction. They turn even the most straightforward pieces of evidence into a battleground of verification and uncertainty.

In corporate settings, face-to-face interactions and voice verification have long been relied on to establish credibility and authorize major transactions. In daily life, people lean on these familiar voices and faces as primary indicators of what's real. This deep pattern of trust, once a strength, has become a weak point that deepfake technology exploits.

When you can generate convincing lies on demand, the boundary between the genuine and the synthetic fades. Individuals and organizations are left navigating a world where the rules for recognizing authenticity no longer hold steady. They face not just confusion, but a profound risk of manipulation and exploitation of decisions made in good faith turning against them, of relationships and reputations becoming collateral in someone else's scheme. It's a landscape where illusions can be made to look as real as the truth itself, and the consequences can be permanent.

With everything becoming so digital, will we be forced to return to in-person meetings? Will people start flying across the country several times a week for face-to-face interactions simply because they can no longer trust digital representations? This is more than a question of convenience; it's a question of security—of being able to look someone in the eye and know they're real.

Beyond Corporate Fraud: The Wider Impact

The implications extend far beyond corporate fraud. Consider, for example:

- In the political arena, deepfake technology has already been used to generate fabricated speeches by world leaders, creating confusion and influencing public perception.
- In law enforcement, there have been cases of criminals using deepfake disguises to evade facial recognition systems, complicating investigations and forensic analysis.
- Even in personal relationships, AI-generated videos and voice recordings have been weaponized in blackmail and defamation cases, demonstrating that no sector is immune to the risks posed by synthetic media.

If a fake CFO can approve multimillion-dollar transfers, what prevents bad actors from presenting falsified testimony in court, impersonating government officials to issue fabricated policies, or even altering the outcome of high-stakes negotiations? What happens when video and audio evidence, once regarded as the final word in truth, become nothing more than another layer of manipulation?

These are not theoretical threats. They are already happening, infiltrating every level of society where trust is required. The success of these scams does not rely on deepfakes being perfect, only on them being convincing enough to override a victim's instinct to hesitate. And in a world moving at breakneck speed, hesitation is a luxury that corporate leaders, law enforcement, and policymakers can no longer afford. The ability to pause, verify, and question is being eroded by the demand for instant decisions, creating an environment where manipulation not only survives but thrives.

A New Kind of Cybercrime

Deepfakes have moved beyond Internet novelties and political misinformation. They are now a fully realized tool for cybercriminals, unlocking an entirely new category of fraud. In traditional scams, criminals relied on deception that was text-based, such as phishing emails, fraudulent invoices, or fabricated documents. Even phone-based scams, such as impersonating bank representatives or government officials, required scammers to rely on persuasion alone. But deepfakes change the equation entirely.

A CEO of a UK-based energy firm learned this lesson the hard way. He received an urgent phone call from his company's German parent, the voice on the other end thick with its familiar accent, instructing him to transfer €220,000 to a Hungarian supplier. The CEO complied without hesitation. The voice was familiar. The request was urgent. And the situation seemed completely legitimate. Only after the money was gone did he realize he had never actually spoken to his boss.

These scams succeed not because they are flawless, but because they exploit trust at its core. Humans heavily rely on recognition, on impossibly small cues that signal familiarity and legitimacy. When a known voice speaks, when a trusted face appears on a screen, doubt is not the default response. The brain works against skepticism, filling in missing details and smoothing over any small irregularities.

I saw this firsthand during my experiments with the Kevin Experiments and how easy it was to trick the mind into believing a fake video or voice was real simply because the right cues were there. I managed to circumvent the recognition gate by leaning on the trust of another person, sort of like the transitive property of trust: if A trusts B and

B trusts C, then A will trust C. Those experiments showed me how criminals can leapfrog skepticism by co-opting existing relationships of trust. Criminals do not need to create deepfakes that can withstand forensic analysis. They only need to produce something believable enough for a few critical moments, long enough for the victim to comply.

Trust Is the New Attack Surface

Deepfake cybercrime proves particularly insidious because of the preparation that goes into it. This is not a random phishing email sent to thousands of addresses in hopes that someone will click. It is a targeted, highly sophisticated operation. Criminals research their targets, compiling video footage, voice recordings, and behavioral cues from publicly available sources. Executives who frequently appear in press interviews, corporate webinars, or investor calls provide scammers with a goldmine of training data. Even casual social media posts, an offhand remark in a company podcast, and even a birthday message in a LinkedIn video can be used to refine AI-generated replicas.

This shift has made deepfake-enabled fraud exponentially more dangerous than previous forms of deception. The cost of entry is low, the tools are widely available, and the risk to criminals is minimal. They do not need to break into a system, hack into bank accounts, or physically steal anything. Instead, they hijack trust itself, inserting false authority into decision-making processes, where victims become the unwitting facilitators of their own financial losses.

In the hands of the right scammer, deepfake technology is a master key, capable of bypassing existing security protocols, social barriers, and institutional checks. Deepfake-enabled fraud constitutes an entirely new category of crime, one that exploits the very ways we interact with people we trust.

There's something uniquely terrifying about realizing that trust, not data, is the new attack surface. It's not your firewalls or encryption that are being bypassed. It's your people. Your systems may be bulletproof, but the human being on the other end of the video call? They are the weak link. And the irony is, that person is doing exactly what they've been trained to do: respond to authority, act quickly, avoid delay.

Executives can invest millions in cybersecurity infrastructure, but if a single employee transfers funds based on a convincing fake voice, all that protection vanishes in seconds. The greatest vulnerability lies in a moment of belief. Once one person is fooled, once one meeting or one message slips past the filters, the ripple effects begin. Colleagues follow suit. Departments react. News spreads. The lie metastasizes, feeding off the organization's own processes. A single moment of deception turns into a story that reprograms how people respond to everything that follows.

This manipulation doesn't stay inside company walls. It reaches courtrooms, public opinion, and national security briefings. Once something appears real enough to act on, the consequences take root immediately. Proving it false later doesn't undo the action it triggered. The damage is immediate. Correction comes too late.

This erosion of trust is not confined to banks, governments, or high-profile CEOs. It influences how people see each other, how decisions are made, and how certainty is defined. One show in particular saw this collapse coming years before most people did.

Human Behavior Is the Weak Link

Mr. Robot, a drama television series that premiered in 2015, built its entire premise on a single truth: the weakest point in any security system isn't the code, it's the human. From the very first episode, Elliot Alderson doesn't hack firewalls. He hacks people. Passwords don't get cracked; they get offered up voluntarily through manipulation, fear, and trust. The series not only makes this salient point but weaponizes it. Every exploit, every breach, every collapse of a corporation or institution in that show hinges on a moment of psychological vulnerability.

This relevance has only intensified in our current moment. What was once fiction is now operational reality. The social engineering tactics Elliot uses, posing as a tech support agent and sending phishing emails, manipulating people into clicking or confessing, have been absorbed, refined, and scaled by AI. Deepfakes are the logical next evolution of that same game. Instead of guessing a password, a convincing video impersonation gets results faster.

Mr. Robot understood that paranoia isn't an anomaly in the system. It's part of the system. The show made it clear that the collapse of trust wasn't a distant possibility. It was a predictable outcome. The tools have changed, but human behavior hasn't. People still believe what they see. They follow what feels familiar. And when trust becomes that easy to replicate, doubt becomes the only defense.

Doubt spreads beyond the immediate victims to everyone else. In the aftermath of a deepfake attack, even those who weren't directly deceived begin to question the integrity of everything around them. Did the assistant verify that call? Did Legal double check that document? Did we really hear what we think we heard? Processes that once felt reliable become suspect, and relationships that once felt secure start to strain. People hesitate. They delay decisions, review everything twice, and rely on extra layers of verification that clog workflows not because of due diligence but because of fear. Cohesion doesn't just suffer. It dissolves.

The breakdown extends beyond corporate operations. It spreads into the institutions designed to hold the line on truth. In courtrooms, deepfakes are testing the limits of what qualifies as evidence. A video confession that might have once been decisive now requires authentication. A phone recording draws skepticism. Judges pause. Juries hesitate. Defense attorneys press the point.

Legal teams increasingly raise the possibility that a piece of video or audio might be fake, not because they have proof, but because the suggestion alone creates doubt. Prosecutors find themselves in a defensive position, forced to validate every frame, every word. The old assumption that video tells the truth has flipped. Now, everything must be proven authentic before it's even considered credible. But we raise the question: Who determines whether the footage is genuine or fake? Who is qualified enough? What software are they using that has been proven to be 100 percent? After all, we are gambling with someone's freedom, and shouldn't we be absolutely sure, beyond the shadow of a doubt, that the person on trial is actually innocent until truly proven guilty?

For those actually guilty, this shift becomes a tool. A politician caught in a damaging recording can claim it's fabricated. A corporate executive under investigation can deny their own voice. The more people hear that deepfakes exist, the easier it becomes to reject inconvenient truths. Accountability blurs. The truth weakens under pressure. The courtroom hesitates rather than collapsing outright. And in hesitation, trust evaporates.

The Lasting Victim Impact

The impact extends beyond reputation and finances—it becomes existential. When someone becomes the target of a deepfake—for example, when their likeness is manipulated and broadcast to the world without consent—the effect is not just reputational or financial. It becomes existential and chips away at the foundation of who they are, how they are perceived, and what they believe to be under their control. This is especially devastating in cases where the deepfakes are sexual in nature, a category that has exploded in both volume and harm. These types of attacks weaponize intimacy, turning a person's image into something deeply violating and nearly impossible to erase. In response, new legislation is emerging specifically to criminalize the creation and distribution of nonconsensual deepfake pornography, but the damage often travels faster than the remedy. For many victims, the emotional fallout arrives long before legal recourse.

For the person being impersonated, there is an immediate sense of violation, like their identity has been hijacked and reassembled into something unfamiliar. They may know the video is fake, their friends and family might believe them, but the rest of the world doesn't operate on certainty. It operates on impressions. And impressions are hard to undo once they take hold.

Even when the truth surfaces and the deception is exposed, the lingering effects don't vanish. Employers hesitate. Partners withdraw. Online comments accumulate. The original video might be taken down, but by then, it has already been screen-recorded, shared, reposted, and embedded in narratives that no longer care whether it's real. The correction becomes a footnote to a much louder fiction.

This is the same uncanny power I tapped into with Myster Giraffe, though from a very different angle. I wasn't shocked when the tools evolved in this direction. I saw it coming. It felt more like an eventuality and less like a surprise. The moment I realized what could be done with a few training clips and the right neural net, it was obvious that others would follow the same path with different intentions. My aim was always to entertain, to craft cultural parodies that were surreal and joyful, never misrepresentative. But it was also clear from the start that the same mechanics could be used to confuse, defraud, or destabilize. That inevitability never left my mind.

So when I see those same techniques being used to erode trust or hijack reputations, I don't feel alarm; it serves as confirmation. This was never a question of if, but when. The line between performance and deception was never especially sturdy. It has always depended on intent, on context, on the viewer's willingness to question what they're shown. What's changed is not the boundary itself but the sheer number of people now crossing it without hesitation. It's like watching drivers speed down a highway without seatbelts simply because everyone else is doing it. There are fatal wrecks happening all around them, but those stories don't make the front page. Is it ignorance? Apathy? Are we failing to grasp the risk, or just accepting it as the new cost of convenience? This normalization creates a precarious moment. The danger operates in full view as society gradually normalizes the risk.

Government Responses

Several governments have begun to respond, but the legal system moves with a different tempo than the Internet. Although some states and countries have passed laws targeting the creation and sharing of sexually explicit deepfakes without consent, enforcement remains a challenge. Platforms struggle to keep up with takedown requests. Jurisdictions disagree on definitions. Unfortunately and unfairly, victims often have to relive their trauma just to prove the content is fake. And in many places, the burden still falls on the person harmed to initiate the process, usually at their own expense.

New legislation is a necessary step, but not a final one. Without broader coordination and tech platform accountability, the legal system risks becoming another institution that acknowledges harm but cannot meaningfully prevent it. The law may eventually catch up, but for many victims, it will always be too late.

At the heart of this evolving landscape is AI itself, driving the creation of deepfakes and the broader wave of digital illusions, from generative voice models to sophisticated social engineering schemes. Although AI is a very useful tool in many industries and methodologies, it's the primary catalyst for every new twist in the story of digital deception and defense. AI's reach extends far beyond these early examples, weaving its way into automated text generation, digital voice cloning, and entire ecosystems of synthetic content that can blur lines and erode trust in an instant. What once required specialized skills and insider knowledge is now widely available and becoming more sophisticated by the day. These transformations are reshaping the balance of power between creator and verifier, and between truth and fiction itself.

The Evolution of Detection Tools

In this dynamic environment, provenance becomes harder to trace. The way we share and consume information across social platforms, through direct messages, and in instant reposts creates a landscape where the origins of content blur and fragment into a fog of half-verified claims. This reflects a core feature of how information now circulates, leaving even the best intentions to vanish into a crowd of echoes. Rather than a flaw, this fluidity reflects the reality of a digital ecosystem that was designed to prioritize reach and engagement over certainty, where speed and volume outpace careful validation and verification.

Beyond high-profile scams, synthetic identities now weave into everyday interactions and scenarios that test our ability to discern reality. From job interviews where fake candidates craft entire personas, to dating profiles designed to exploit vulnerable moments of connection, these digital personas reshape trust across all levels of engagement and social interaction. Dating profiles in particular have become a ripe area for this new wave of manipulation. They have evolved into a kind of supercharged catfishing with stakes that climb ever higher as scammers use romance as the perfect pretext to separate an unwitting victim from their money or sensitive information.

These are not isolated incidents but part of a broader shift where the same generative tools that create a convincing deepfake can build entire digital identities out of thin air. They can replicate voices, mimic gestures, and craft social footprints that blend seamlessly into real conversations, changing the stakes of every digital exchange and testing our instincts for authenticity in ways that challenge our most basic social interactions.

Here's some good news, though: detection tools have come a long way. Researchers have developed techniques that can analyze subtle inconsistencies in facial movements, lighting, and even biological signals like heart rate reflected in skin tone. Some systems look for the fingerprints of specific AI models, and others rely on entropy patterns that are invisible to the human eye. These methods show promise in controlled environments. But out in the wild, where videos are compressed, filtered, distorted, and reshared across endless platforms, those signals are often lost. It's a reactive game, constantly trying to catch up. And although these techniques are a step forward, they're still playing by rules written after the fact. The proactive countermeasures? That's what the next chapter is about.

A convincing fake can go viral in minutes, but the verification process may take hours, sometimes days, and by then, the damage is already done. The headline has landed. The public has moved on. The correction, if it comes at all, enters a dead conversation that's already shifted past the truth.

The Evolution of Access: From Experts to Anyone

When DeepFaceLab first emerged, it lived on a single GitHub page that was almost a secret society in itself. Most people didn't even know what GitHub was, much less how to navigate it. The software demanded a powerful NVIDIA GPU, an understanding of batch scripts, and a willingness to wrestle with a poorly translated Russian-to-English manual. It wasn't for the faint of heart. It was a challenge only a tiny subset of the population could even attempt.

My own edge came from years of working in visual effects, where using computers to composite, animate, and refine digital illusions was second nature. For most people, what they saw as a finished product was just my starting point. DeepFaceLab could do some crude compositing, but it was nowhere near the level of polish I could achieve using industry-standard tools honed over 15 years. But that was then. Now, the tools have evolved beyond those niche circles.

Today, anyone with a smartphone and ten dollars a month can create a convincing fake. These services have moved to the cloud, stripping away the need for expensive hardware or industry-specific knowledge. The barrier to entry is practically gone. Technical skill has given way to simple curiosity, access, and the willingness to click Generate. What was once a craft has become a service, offered to anyone who wants to shape the truth to their own advantage. Not only does this shift lower the threshold for entry; it erases it entirely, changing the landscape of authenticity in ways that go far beyond what the earliest creators imagined, all while increasing the opportunities for bad actors to try their hand at AI-powered deception at scale

This imbalance—the speed of creation outpacing the speed of detection—is what makes the deepfake threat so uniquely difficult. We are not dealing with a stable opponent. We're dealing with a shape-shifting ecosystem where the rules change as soon as you write them down. And in that kind of environment, even the best detection tools feel like sandbags against a flood. The truth hasn't lost its value. But it's lost its urgency.

It's like a high-stakes duel between a master jewel thief and a relentless detective: two professionals circling each other across time, each adapting, each refining. The thief pulls off a flawless heist, and the detective tightens their methods in response. They don't just make each other better; they continually define and redefine the terms of the game. This becomes a test of endurance rather than a single decisive battle.

The speed of creation outpacing the speed of detection makes the deepfake threat so uniquely difficult. We're dealing with a shape-shifting ecosystem where the rules change as soon as you write them down.

The same dynamic plays out here. The deepfake creator gets sharper. The detector gets smarter. Then the creator pivots again. Back and forth, iron sharpening iron. But it's not a game anyone wins. It's a cycle, an unending sequence of escalation and adaptation. The technology doesn't settle. It evolves.

At some point in the fight against computer viruses, the hackers pivoted. Not because they were defeated, but because the game changed. Antivirus software got faster. Sandboxing became standard, and threat modeling matured. The low-hanging fruit was gone, so attackers moved to easier, more profitable grifts like phishing, ransomware, and social engineering. The arms race didn't end; it simply shifted terrain.

This is no different. Deepfakes will keep evolving until the energy behind them either burns out or finds a new outlet. One side innovates. The other adapts. This arms race is more than a clash of tools; it's a test of authenticity itself. Every deepfake, every countermeasure, every shift in tactics underscores a deeper truth in the digital age: what's real is no longer self-evident. It's an active decision, a standard that must be earned and re-earned with every new advancement. The shape of authenticity is no longer fixed. It's dynamic, shifting with each pivot and counter. That's the paradox we're left with: authenticity, the foundation of trust, is now the most contested territory in our information landscape. The marathon continues.

What's Next?

As I write this, new AI models are being released monthly, each more sophisticated than the last. Within the next two years, we'll likely see deepfakes that can fool even advanced detection systems, real-time voice cloning from just seconds of audio, and AI that can generate entire fictional personas complete with social media histories and behavioral patterns.

For businesses, this means building adaptive defenses rather than static ones. The companies that survive the next wave won't be those with the best current detection tools but those with human-centered protocols flexible enough to evolve. Think of it like cybersecurity: you don't just install antivirus software once and forget about it. You create systems that can identify new threats and respond quickly. The same principle applies here.

What comes next is less about speed and more about structure. As the tools keep changing, so must the systems meant to contain them. The next chapter looks at the frameworks—legal, ethical, and institutional—trying to catch up. It's about how societies respond when the ground shifts beneath them, and what it means to create accountability in a world where proof itself is no longer obvious.

Chapter 6

Proactive Solutions: Staying Ahead of the Curve

The evidence is clear about this one fact: deepfakes change what we believe and redefine reality itself. We've seen millions stolen, blackmail executed, and legal systems compromised, but these are only previews of what's to come. The question now isn't whether deepfakes will deceive us. They already have. The real question is, what can we do to fight back and protect our sense of trust?

Not all deepfake scams succeed. The only difference between those who fall for them and those who do not is whether someone takes the extra step to verify the truth in real time.

Jennifer DeStefano was almost one of the victims. In early 2023, she answered a phone call from an unknown number while standing outside a music studio. On the other end, her 15-year-old daughter, Briana, was sobbing and crying for help. "Mom, help me! These bad men have me," the voice pleaded. It captured every nuance, inflection, and emotional detail that only a mother would recognize.

Then a man's voice took over the call. He demanded a ransom, threatening to harm Briana and take her to Mexico if Jennifer did not comply. The panic was immediate. Jennifer was convinced her daughter had been kidnapped. But before she could comply with the demand, a friend standing nearby urged her to call her husband to verify Briana's whereabouts. With shaking hands, she made the call, and within moments, her husband confirmed that Briana was safe at home, completely unaware of what was happening.

The scam had failed. Not because the deepfake wasn't convincing. Not because Jennifer wasn't terrified. It failed because she stopped to verify the truth in real time.

This is the difference between those who are scammed and those who are not. The individuals and organizations that implement real-time verification, whether through personal skepticism, corporate safeguards, or technological countermeasures, are the ones that avoid catastrophe. The Jennifer DeStefano case is proof that *real-time checks* are the deciding factor between deception and security.

The same principle applies at scale. If a CEO stops to verify a financial request before wiring millions of dollars, fraud fails. If a company implements a security system that automatically verifies the authenticity of video calls, deepfake scams never reach their targets. If the Internet itself had built-in safeguards against synthetic manipulation, the viral spread of fake content could be halted before it ever gained traction.

This is where SawStop and *Inject, Measure, Verify* come in.

Lessons from SawStop: Preventing Disaster Before It Happens

In the late 1990s, Steve Gass, a physicist and woodworking enthusiast, stood at the crossroads of tragedy and innovation. Thousands of people each year suffered devastating injuries from table saw accidents. For many, it was more than a physical loss. It was the end of livelihoods, careers, and independence. To Gass, these injuries were not inevitable. They were preventable. The solution came to him in a flash of brilliance, rooted in simplicity and science.

Gass knew that the problem stemmed from human error and the lack of a fail-safe mechanism in one of the most dangerous tools in the world. He theorized that if the saw could recognize human contact the moment it happened, it could prevent serious injury.

What followed was relentless experimentation, calculations, and prototype designs that eventually led to one of the most important safety innovations in modern manufacturing.

His invention, SawStop, was as elegant in its execution as it was in its design. A small electrical signal was sent through the saw blade, and as long as the blade spun through wood, the signal remained stable. But if the blade touched human skin, which conducts electricity differently, the signal would change. In an instant, faster than the blink of an eye, a spring-loaded brake would deploy, stopping the blade before it could sever a finger. The entire process took less than five milliseconds, faster than the human brain could even register pain. The brilliance of the mechanism was that it did not require complex artificial intelligence, sensors, or redundant systems. It worked on a fundamental, immutable principle of physics.

But innovation alone was not enough. Gass faced resistance from established tool manufacturers that were hesitant to disrupt the industry or increase production costs. He fought battles in patent courts and regulatory agencies, proving that the safety of millions of workers was worth more than industry inertia. His perseverance paid off. SawStop became a revolutionary force in woodworking safety, transforming an industry that had been stagnant in its approach to accident prevention for over a century.

SawStop technology detects human contact and stops the blade in under five milliseconds.

Proactive Solutions: Staying Ahead of the Curve

Over the years, SawStop has prevented tens of thousands of life-altering injuries. Carpenters, hobbyists, and professionals alike owe their hands, and sometimes their lives, to a system that fundamentally changed how table saws worked. Its brilliance lay not in complexity but in its simplicity. It did not try to overanalyze the problem. It focused on what mattered, detecting an anomaly and stopping harm before it could occur.

SawStop's genius was not just in its function but in the way it redefined responsibility. It did not put the burden on the user to avoid mistakes. It assumed mistakes would happen and built a mechanism that would prevent catastrophe regardless of human error. It understood the inevitability of failure and responded with a system that made failure inconsequential.

Inject, Measure, Verify: The Real-time Deepfake Kill Switch

This concept is what makes a method I developed called *Inject, Measure, Verify* not just useful but revolutionary in its own right. The parallel is clear. Just as SawStop did not try to change the way people used saws but instead rethought safety itself, Inject, Measure, Verify does not attempt to police deepfake manipulation after the fact. It builds authentication into the digital framework from the start, assuming that bad actors will attempt to manipulate data and creating a system that invalidates tampered content before harm can be done.

Where SawStop recognized the unchangeable nature of human reflex and built a safeguard around it, Inject, Measure, Verify recognizes the inevitability of synthetic media and builds authenticity directly into the fabric of communication. It is proactive rather than reactive, stopping the deception before it has the chance to spread, just as SawStop stops the blade before it can injure.

The lesson here concerns safety mechanisms and represents a fundamental shift in thinking. It is not enough to detect deception after it happens. The only way to stay ahead of AI-driven fraud is to create systems where fraud becomes functionally impossible to execute successfully. SawStop did not make better saw operators. It made saws that prevented failure before the operator could even react. Inject, Measure, Verify follows the same principle, stopping digital fraud at the root rather than cleaning up the mess afterward.

This same philosophy of simplicity and fail-safe design drives the solution to an entirely different crisis: the rise of real-time deepfake manipulation.

The concept behind Inject, Measure, Verify is as straightforward as it is revolutionary. Instead of analyzing millions of pixels after content has already been created, this system embeds a unique, entropy-based fingerprint into the digital stream itself (see Figure 6.1). This fingerprint serves as a continuous authenticity check, making it impossible for deepfake alterations to go unnoticed.

The fingerprint is generated from naturally occurring randomness, such as the chaotic movement of a lava lamp or the unpredictable

Figure 6.1 The real-time deepfake kill-switch architecture

Proactive Solutions: Staying Ahead of the Curve

fluctuations in thermal noise. These are phenomena no computer, no matter how powerful, can perfectly predict or replicate. Even quantum-level AI cannot reconstruct these entropy-based signatures. This results in a dynamic watermark that is not only impossible to replicate but remains bound to the video stream itself, acting as an unforgeable signature.

This principle is not without precedent. In the late 1990s, researchers at Silicon Graphics pioneered a unique approach to randomness in cryptographic security known as LavaRand. The concept was simple yet profound. By capturing images of lava lamps in motion and extracting entropy from their unpredictable patterns, the researchers could generate cryptographic keys that were functionally impossible to replicate. LavaRand leveraged a fundamental truth of physics: natural randomness is ungovernable and outside the predictive power of any algorithm.

Today, LavaRand is still in active use, with Cloudflare utilizing a wall of lava lamps in its headquarters to generate highly secure cryptographic keys. This real-world application underscores how effective natural entropy is in creating unbreakable security mechanisms. Inject, Measure, Verify borrows from this same idea, applying it to digital media authentication. By anchoring a unique, entropy-based signature to video and audio content, this method ensures that each transmission is an unalterable stream of verified truth.

Once the fingerprint is embedded, the system continuously monitors its integrity at every frame, every second. It functions like a silent, ever-present security layer. If someone attempts to tamper with the stream, whether by injecting a deepfake via a virtual webcam, altering the video feed in real time, or applying generative AI filters, the fingerprint is corrupted. IMV instantly detects the change, much like how SawStop recognizes the moment human skin touches the blade. And just as SawStop activates its brake in milliseconds to prevent a catastrophic injury, Inject, Measure, Verify responds immediately, flagging the compromised content or shutting down the transmission before the manipulation has a chance to do harm.

The power of this system is that it does not require new infrastructure to function. The technology already exists. Webcams, streaming platforms, and content delivery networks can integrate this method with minimal modification. Unlike bloated machine learning models that attempt to detect fakes after the fact, Inject, Measure, Verify stops manipulation at its source by ensuring that every frame of every video maintains a verifiable and untampered fingerprint. It does not attempt to interpret the content of an image or video. It simply ensures that whatever is transmitted is exactly what was originally recorded.

This approach is not just a technological leap but a philosophical one. It acknowledges that deepfake threats are no longer theoretical or rare. They are here, evolving rapidly, and will soon reach a point where the average person will have no way of distinguishing truth from fiction. The only viable solution is to bake authenticity directly into the fabric of digital communication, making manipulation detectable before it ever reaches the public eye.

Additionally, Inject, Measure, Verify does not attempt to play cat and mouse with bad actors. It does not require AI arms races to continuously evolve detection methods. Instead, it establishes an immutable baseline of truth, much like SawStop created an immutable safeguard against human error in woodworking.

The implications are vast:

Where SawStop addressed a fundamental flaw in tool safety, Inject, Measure, Verify addresses the most fundamental flaw in digital media today: the absence of built-in verification. It turns authentication into a live, unbreakable process, rather than a game of forensic guesswork.

- Governments could embed Inject, Measure, Verify into their official press conferences, ensuring that every statement made by a world leader is confirmed as unaltered.

- Financial institutions could use this method to verify video-based identity authentication, preventing fraud before it occurs.

- Social media platforms could integrate this into live streams, ensuring that fake broadcasts cannot gain traction before they spread misinformation.

This system is not a moonshot. It is not an abstract theoretical construct. It is an achievable, practical safeguard against a digital world that is growing more deceptive by the day. Just as SawStop became the industry standard for saw safety, Inject, Measure, Verify has the potential to become the universal standard for digital media authentication.

The choice is clear. The world can either continue reacting to deception after it happens, or it can build a system where deception never has a chance to take hold.

While Inject, Measure, Verify provides a technological foundation for authenticity, technology alone is not enough to stop the spread of deepfakes. People must remain skeptical and aware. Deepfake scams succeed not just because of advanced AI but because humans are wired to trust what they see and hear. This is why social engineering, which exploits human psychology, is just as dangerous as the technology itself.

I know this sounds complex, but implementing these kinds of safeguards doesn't require a complete infrastructure overhaul. Start small: audit your current communication channels and identify the highest-risk touchpoints—usually anything involving financial authorization or sensitive data transfer. Then layer in verification requirements proportional to the risk. A $500 purchase might only need email confirmation, but a $50,000 wire transfer should require multiple verification methods, including in-person or previously established protocols. The goal isn't to eliminate all risk—it's to make your organization a harder target than the business next door.

The Power of Simple Safeguards

In an era where a convincing voice or video can trigger multimillion-dollar transactions, businesses must fundamentally rethink how they verify identities and secure communications. Deepfake fraud targets individuals and threatens entire corporate structures, exploiting weak points in verification protocols and human trust. The lessons learned from past fraud cases make it clear that traditional security measures are no longer sufficient.

At the heart of business security is verification. Historically, companies have relied on simple methods like passwords, voice recognition, or visual confirmation through video calls. But deepfake technology has made these methods less reliable. A CEO's voice can be cloned from a short audio clip found online. A face can be replicated with astonishing accuracy using AI-generated video. The stakes are high, but that does not mean the solutions have to be complicated.

Sometimes the simplest solutions are the most effective. Think of it like locking your front door. Sure, you could install a high-tech security system with cameras and alarms, but often, a strong lock and a good habit of using it consistently will keep you just as safe. The same principle applies to protecting your business from deepfake fraud.

Personal Code Words

Let me set the stage for you. In the midst of rising deepfake scams and a world increasingly vulnerable to AI-driven deception, cybersecurity expert Cody Barrow has emerged as a thoughtful voice of caution and practical action. As the chief executive of EclecticIQ and a former advisor to the U.S. government, Barrow knows firsthand how these threats evolve. In his own home, he and his wife created a secret password, a low-tech but powerful safeguard to protect themselves from deepfake impersonation.

A simple code word could save your company's resources or your personal assets. It could be a shared memory from a family trip, the name of a childhood pet, or even a tiny scar or birthmark known only to close friends. Anything unique to you can serve as a password. These little details of life can become your shield, reinforcing the most critical truth of this digital age: trust must be earned and guarded, always. This tactic is deceptively simple but remarkably effective because it relies on a personal bond. It also taps into something deeper: a sense of trust that no algorithm can fake, a whisper shared only in the most private moments.

Barrow's advice comes at a time when AI-powered scams are exploiting our most basic instincts to trust familiar voices and faces. By establishing a private keyword or phrase, you introduce an extra layer of defense that technology alone cannot provide. In a world where synthetic voices and faces can fool even the sharpest observer, this simple step can mean the difference between safety and disaster. It is not just a clever trick; it is a recognition of the most human form of verification, shared memory and personal history.

So take a moment: do you have a code word? Who knows it? What story would you choose as your secret shield? It is a small effort that can protect not only your money, but also your peace of mind and the quiet confidence that comes from knowing you are prepared.

Imagine getting a late-night video call from your son asking for an urgent money transfer to cover bail. Would you remember to ask for the code word before sending thousands of dollars? Or picture a scenario where your trusted business partner emails you to release funds to a new supplier. If they cannot supply the phrase you agreed on, that one question could save your company's resources.

I remember having my wallet stolen years ago. The thief had my ID and banking details, and they nearly drained my account. Since then, I have asked my bank to put a verbal password in place for every transaction. Even I must use this password each time, and over

15 years later, it is still in place. It may seem low-tech, but that single word is my shield. It is not just a password; it is a lesson in how trust should be managed and defended. I recommend that everyone adopt this simple practice. It is not only a barrier for bad actors but a constant reminder to protect what matters.

Slow It Down

Another effective approach is to slow things down. Scammers rely on creating a sense of urgency to bypass your natural skepticism. Implementing a cooling-off period for large transactions or sensitive decisions can be a game-changer. Requiring a second person to verify a request, even if it is just a quick phone call, can stop fraud in its tracks. Think of it as the business equivalent of looking both ways before crossing the street.

Encouraging a culture of verification within your organization is key. Make it normal to double-check requests, even if they seem to come from trusted sources. A simple habit of pausing to ask, "Does this feel right?" can be incredibly powerful. Train employees to recognize red flags like unusual requests, changes in communication patterns, or anything that seems slightly off. It is not about being paranoid. It is about being mindful and creating a system of shared vigilance that keeps everyone safe.

For example, imagine you receive an urgent email that looks like it is from your CEO, asking you to wire a large sum of money for an emergency payment. Instead of rushing to comply, pick up the phone and verify the request directly. Or picture a scenario where a vendor emails to update their bank details. Before updating payment information, confirm the change through a separate channel or with a trusted contact. These real-world examples highlight how a brief pause and a simple phone call can be the difference between falling for a scam and staying secure.

But let's also consider the reality of working in an office environment, where hierarchy and fear of offending superiors can cloud judgment. Employees might hesitate to question a request that appears to come from the CEO, fearing they will be seen as insubordinate or overly cautious. This is exactly the environment scammers exploit, where it feels awkward to ask direct questions.

The key is to create a culture where asking for confirmation is seen as diligence, not disrespect. One of the best ways to build that culture is to encourage team-building and strong connections between coworkers. When your team knows each other better, they can develop insider memory-led verification practices, naturally weaving these secure habits into their everyday work. Strengthening those bonds makes your team more resilient and better equipped to spot anything out of place.

So, how do you navigate that without upsetting the balance? Frame the verification as a routine part of security, not as doubt about leadership. Try questions like, "I just want to double-check this with you directly before proceeding," or "Can you confirm this is the right amount?" These small adjustments in language can lower the emotional barrier while still doing the critical work of verification.

Importantly, not all solutions require advanced technology or massive financial investments. These simple, low-tech practices create a strong foundation. As deepfake technology becomes more sophisticated, additional safeguards can make the difference between catching a threat early and dealing with its consequences later.

Imagine this: a mid-level employee receives a video call from the company's CFO. The face looks right, the voice sounds perfect, and the sense of urgency is overwhelming. An emergency wire transfer needs to happen immediately, with no time for formalities or questions. But this time, the company's Inject, Measure, Verify system is active. As the employee listens and begins to comply, this method quietly injects a verification signal into the call. It measures and finds no matching response from the supposed CFO. A warning flashes on the employee's screen, alerting them that the video is likely a deepfake. The employee pauses and asks the CFO to provide the shared passphrase they had agreed on as a secondary check. When the fake CFO hesitates and stumbles, the employee knows for sure it's a scam. "IMV" and the human instinct work together to reveal the deception. This time, the money stays where it belongs, and the employee is both protected and empowered.

This is where technologies like Inject, Measure, Verify prove invaluable. Although human awareness is crucial, having automated systems that constantly monitor for authenticity adds another layer of defense. Think of it as fastening your seatbelt. You don't expect to crash every time you drive, but if something does go wrong, you'll be glad you did.

Because as powerful as technology can be, it's not the only line of defense. The next challenge isn't just about stopping machines, but more about understanding people, and that's where the real battle begins.

When the Law Isn't Enough: Protecting Your Business from Deepfake Liability

Although technology and awareness can reduce the risks of deepfake fraud, businesses also need to understand the legal landscape surrounding this evolving threat. Laws often lag behind technological advancements, leaving companies exposed to risks they may not even recognize. Regulations addressing deepfakes vary by country, and enforcement is inconsistent at best. The reality is that legislative protection does not guarantee practical security, and in many cases, the burden of protection still falls on businesses.

Legal systems are slow-moving by nature, and deepfakes evolve too quickly for lawmakers to keep pace. Even when new legislation is passed, enforcement is often fragmented. A law that applies in one jurisdiction may have no impact in another, and many legal definitions struggle to keep up with the technical complexity of AI-driven fraud. Companies operating across multiple countries face an even greater challenge, as compliance with one region's regulations does not guarantee protection in another.

One of the biggest challenges in deepfake-related fraud is jurisdiction. A fraudster in Nigeria uses AI tools to impersonate a London-based CFO, tricking a finance team in New York into transferring millions to a Hong Kong account. This creates a legal gray area where companies struggle to determine where and how to take action. Unlike traditional financial fraud, where banks and institutions have well-defined protocols, deepfake fraud does not fit neatly into existing legal frameworks. Without international cooperation, prosecuting offenders remains incredibly difficult. Many cybercriminals operate from jurisdictions where enforcement is weak, knowing that even if they are identified, extradition and prosecution are unlikely.

Another issue is corporate liability. If a company is impersonated through a deepfake scam, who is responsible for the financial loss? If an employee uses deepfake technology to manipulate internal communications, is the company legally at fault? The answer depends on the legal jurisdiction, but most businesses do not yet have policies in place to address these concerns. Without clear legal guidance, businesses need to take proactive steps to protect themselves. Some companies have already begun including deepfake-specific liability clauses in their cybersecurity insurance policies, recognizing that traditional coverage may not account for AI-generated fraud.

However, these policies vary widely, and many businesses may find themselves unprotected when an attack occurs.

One way to do this is by incorporating deepfake clauses into contracts and policies. These can outline verification procedures for communications, financial transactions, and public-facing content. Companies should also establish internal response teams trained to handle potential deepfake incidents. Having a documented policy on authentication and verification not only strengthens security but also provides a legal defense if fraud does occur. Companies should also consider adopting industry-wide security standards for verifying media authenticity, similar to how financial institutions use standardized fraud detection protocols to prevent wire fraud.

Another challenge businesses face is proving damages in court. Even if a deepfake scam results in financial loss, a company must provide sufficient evidence that the fraud was caused by manipulated media. Courts often require forensic analysis, expert testimony, and digital traceability to confirm that a deepfake was responsible for the damages incurred. As AI-generated content becomes more advanced, proving that a video, audio recording, or document has been altered can become a complex and expensive process. Businesses must maintain digital records and forensic audit trails to provide verifiable proof in legal disputes, ensuring that they can substantiate claims of deepfake-related fraud.

As regulations surrounding deepfakes continue to evolve, businesses must take matters into their own hands. Whether you're a global brand or a small company with a dozen employees, the threat is real and personal. The illusion doesn't have to be perfect to be persuasive, and one well-placed fake can undo years of trust in an instant. Ignoring the problem will not make it go away.

Instead, companies must stay informed, implement internal safeguards, and treat deepfake security as an essential part of risk management. Governments may be playing catch-up, but businesses cannot afford to wait. The best protection is preparation, and those who take action now will be far better positioned to navigate the deepfake era than those who choose to react later. This concerns safeguarding your bottom line, name, team, and trust, because when the illusion looks perfect, only the prepared will know the difference.

What's Next?

The fight against deepfake deception requires both technology and vigilance. And that begins with understanding how we, as humans, become targets. In the next chapter, I explore how scammers use deepfakes to exploit human weaknesses, why critical thinking is the strongest defense against AI deception, and how to train yourself to recognize manipulation before it fools you.

From Theory to Practice: Your 90-Day Implementation Guide

The morning after my Sinatra experiment, I woke up with a peculiar feeling. It wasn't just the adrenaline of pulling off something audacious—it was the sobering realization that I had proven how unprepared we all are. If I could fool experts whose job was to catch people like me, what did that say about the rest of us?

That's when I started thinking differently about deepfake defense. It's not enough to understand the problem or even know the solutions exist. You have to actually build the defenses. And building defenses, I learned, is less about buying the right software and more about changing how people think.

This chapter is about that transition—from knowing what you should do to actually doing it. It's a roadmap, but not the kind that gets you from Point A to Point B in a straight line. It's more like a trail map for hiking in unfamiliar territory. You know the destination, but you need to watch your footing, pace yourself, and be ready to adapt when the terrain changes.

The First 30 Days: Foundation Building

Implementation doesn't start with technology. It starts with a conversation.

I remember the first time I tried to explain deepfake risks to a corporate security team. I walked in with slides full of technical specs and detection algorithms, ready to dazzle them with the complexity of the threat. Five minutes in, I could see their eyes glazing over. That's when I realized my mistake: I was solving the wrong problem.

They didn't need to understand how deepfakes work. They needed to understand why their current assumptions about trust were dangerous. So I put away the slides and told them about the finance worker in Hong Kong. About the CEO who lost €220,000 to a familiar voice. About the moment when "seeing is believing" stopped being reliable.

That's your starting point, too. Before you buy a single piece of detection software or write a single policy, you need to have the conversation about why this matters. Not in a conference room with PowerPoint, but in the break room, over coffee, with the people who make the decisions that matter.

Week One

Week One is about asking the right questions. Who in your organization can authorize financial transfers? How do they currently verify those requests? What would happen if someone convincing called, pretending to be your CEO? The answers to these questions will tell you more about your vulnerabilities than any security audit.

I worked with a mid-sized manufacturing company last year that discovered their entire accounts payable process hinged on recognizing voices over the phone. "We've known each other for years," the controller told me. "I'd recognize my boss anywhere." Two weeks later, I played him a deepfake of his boss's voice requesting a routine vendor payment. He authorized it immediately.

That's not a failure of training. That's a failure of assumption. We assume familiarity equals security. We assume that the way we've always done things will continue to work. Deepfakes break those assumptions, which is why your first month isn't about implementing new systems—it's about questioning old ones.

Week Two

You should have mapped your organization's trust ecosystem. Who trusts whom? What communications channels carry the highest risk? Where are the single points of failure? This is more than a technical exercise—it's an anthropological one. You're studying the social patterns that hold your business together so you can identify where they might be exploited.

The personal code word system I described in Chapter 6 is your first practical implementation, and it's where most organizations should start. Not because it's the most sophisticated defense, but because it's the most human one. It forces people to think differently about verification without asking them to learn new technology.

But here's what I've learned about implementing code words: the system only works if everyone buys into the philosophy behind it. If people see it as security theater—something they have to do to check a box—they'll find ways around it. If they understand it as a shared responsibility for protecting something they care about, they'll guard it fiercely.

Week Three

Build buy-in. Share stories. Show examples. Let people see what happens when verification fails. But more importantly, let them feel what happens when it succeeds. When someone remembers to ask for the code word and catches a potential scam, celebrate it. Make verification feel like competence, not paranoia.

Week Four

Your first stress test. Not a formal red team exercise—that comes later—but informal challenges to your new thinking. Have someone call, claiming to be from IT, requesting password resets. Send emails

From Theory to Practice: Your 90-Day Implementation Guide

that look like they're from executives asking for urgent information. See who remembers to pause. See who remembers to verify.

The goal isn't to catch people failing. It's to reinforce the habit of questioning. Because in 60 days, when you're implementing more sophisticated defenses, that habit will be the foundation that everything else builds on.

Days 31–60: System Implementation

By now, your team understands why verification matters. They've practiced the basics. They've internalized the idea that familiar doesn't always mean safe. Now comes the harder part: building systems that support those instincts instead of overriding them.

This is where most organizations get it backward. They buy the most advanced detection software they can afford and assume it will solve the problem. But technology without process is just expensive noise. And a process without culture is just bureaucracy that people work around. The sweet spot is what I call *augmented instinct*—technology that amplifies human judgment rather than replacing it.

When I consult with businesses on choosing detection tools, the first question I ask isn't about accuracy rates or processing speed. It's about workflow integration. How will this tool fit into the way your people actually work? Will it slow them down so much that they'll find ways to bypass it? Will it generate so many false positives that they'll start ignoring its warnings? The best detection system in the world is useless if nobody trusts it.

Week Five

Now you move into vendor evaluation, but not the way you might expect. Don't start with feature comparisons or price negotiations. Start with pilot testing. Most reputable vendors will let you run a limited trial with real content from your organization. Use that trial to test integration, not just accuracy.

Watch how your team responds to the tool. Do they understand its outputs? Do they trust its recommendations? Do they know what to do when it flags something as suspicious? The answers to these questions matter more than benchmark scores on standardized test sets.

Week Six

This is where the "slow it down" principle from Chapter 6 becomes operational. You're not trying to prevent every possible attack—you're trying to create enough friction that most attacks fail and the rest get noticed.

For financial transactions, that might mean mandatory second-person verification for anything over a certain threshold. For sensitive communications, it might mean confirmation through a separate channel. For executive requests, it might mean callback verification using previously established phone numbers.

The key is proportional response. A $100 office supply purchase doesn't need the same verification as a $100,000 wire transfer. But both should have some verification requirements, because the goal is to create a culture where verification is normal.

This is where those conversations from Week One pay off. You're not imposing arbitrary rules from above. You're codifying the defensive instincts your team has already developed.

Weeks Seven and Eight

You should be ready to begin integration testing. You're running your new processes alongside your old ones, looking for friction points and failure modes. Where do people get frustrated? Where do they find workarounds? Where does the system break down under real-world pressure?

Expect resistance. Change is hard, even when people understand why it's necessary. But also expect creativity. Your team will find ways to make the new systems work that you never would have thought of. Listen to those suggestions. The best security protocols are the ones that grow organically from the people who have to use them.

By the end of Month Two, verification shouldn't feel like an extra step—it should feel like due diligence.

Days 61–90: Testing and Refinement

Month Three is when things get interesting. You've built the foundation. You've implemented the systems. Now comes the moment of truth: can your defenses actually stop a determined attacker?

This is where I learned one of the most important lessons about security: the difference between knowing something works in theory and proving it works in practice. I thought I understood this from my years in visual effects—you can plan a shot perfectly, but you don't really know if it works until you see it on screen. Security is the same way, except the stakes are higher and the audience is trying to break your work instead of just watching it.

Week Nine

It's now time to progress into controlled testing, and I can't stress enough how important the word "controlled" is here. You're not trying to break your own systems for sport. You're trying to find and exploit the weak points before someone else does.

Start small. Have a trusted colleague attempt to social engineer information using techniques you've discussed. Call the front desk pretending to be a vendor who needs updated banking information. Send an email that looks like it's from your CEO asking for employee information. See what happens.

The first time I did this kind of testing with a client, I was shocked by how quickly their defenses crumbled. Not because the technology failed—the detection software worked perfectly. But because, when faced with a convincing story and a sense of urgency, people defaulted to helpfulness instead of skepticism.

A "vendor" called, claiming there was a problem with their payment that needed to be resolved immediately. The accounting team knew they should verify the request, but the caller had enough legitimate information to seem credible. And when he said, "I'm about to miss a critical deadline because of this," their instinct to help overrode their training to verify.

That's the gap between policy and practice. Your Week Nine testing will find that gap in your organization. Don't be discouraged when you find it. Better to discover these vulnerabilities in a controlled environment than during a real attack.

Week Ten

Now is the time to test pattern recognition. After your initial tests, you'll start to see where your defenses hold and where they bend. Maybe your technical controls are solid, but your human processes have holes. Maybe your verification requirements are too cumbersome for daily operations. Maybe your team understands the rules but not the principles behind them.

Each vulnerability you find is a chance to strengthen your system. But here's what I've learned: don't try to fix everything at once. Security that's too rigid breaks under real-world pressure. Instead, focus on the highest-impact improvements—the changes that close the biggest gaps with the least disruption.

Sometimes the best fix isn't a new rule. It's better communication about why the existing rules matter. I worked with a company whose employees kept bypassing the verification process for "urgent" requests. Instead of adding more verification steps, we changed how they thought about urgency. Real emergencies are rare, and they usually come with multiple indicators. A single phone call claiming urgency is probably not an emergency. It's more likely to be someone trying to bypass your defenses.

Week Eleven

Time to stress-test under realistic conditions. This is where you simulate not just individual attacks but the kind of coordinated campaigns that real bad actors use. Multiple fake requests from different channels. Pressure tactics combined with technical deception. Social engineering that builds on previous intelligence gathering.

This kind of testing requires more sophistication, and you might want to bring in outside help. But even simple scenarios can be revealing. What happens when your CEO is traveling and someone calls, claiming to be them? What happens when multiple people receive similar requests on the same day? What happens when the attack comes during your busiest period, when everyone is stressed and rushing?

The goal shouldn't be to try to create an impenetrable fortress. Focus on making your organization resilient enough that attacks are more likely to fail than succeed, and when they do succeed, the damage is contained.

Week Twelve

Document and record knowledge transfer. By now, you've learned things about your organization's security posture that nobody knew three months ago. You've identified vulnerabilities, tested solutions, and refined processes. All of that knowledge needs to be captured and shared.

But documentation in security is about creating institutional memory that survives personnel changes. The person who understands your deepfake defenses best shouldn't be the only person who understands them. Knowledge that lives in one person's head is a single point of failure.

Create playbooks, but make them living documents. Security landscapes change too quickly for static procedures. Instead of rigid checklists, create decision frameworks that help people think through novel situations. Instead of comprehensive threat catalogs, create pattern recognition guides that help people spot new variations on old attacks.

Ongoing: Maintenance and Evolution

Three months in, you might think you're done. You've built awareness, implemented systems, and tested your defenses. Your organization is more prepared for deepfake threats than it was 90 days ago. That's worth celebrating.

But if there's one thing I've learned from years in both visual effects and AI, it's that standing still is falling behind. The technology that creates deepfakes doesn't pause for your implementation timeline. The bad actors using this technology don't wait for you to finish your defenses before evolving their attacks.

Monthly reviews become your early warning system. Formal audits have their place, but they're too slow for this threat landscape. I'm talking about informal conversations with your team about what they're seeing, what feels different, and what's making them uncomfortable.

Some of the best threat intelligence I've gotten has come from casual conversations. A receptionist mentioning that they've been getting weird calls. An accountant noting that vendor requests seem more sophisticated lately. A manager feeling like something was off about a video call, even though they couldn't put their finger on what.

These observations don't make it into formal security reports, but they're often the first indicators of evolving threats. Create space for people to share these instincts without having to justify them with hard evidence.

Quarterly assessments are where you step back and look at the bigger picture. What's changed in the threat landscape? What new tools are available? How have your business processes evolved, and do your security measures still fit?

This is also when you evaluate your technology investments. Detection tools that were state-of-the-art six months ago might be obsolete today. Vendors you dismissed earlier might have solved their integration problems. New threats might require different defensive approaches.

But be careful not to chase every new development. The goal isn't to have the newest tools, but to have tools that work for your organization. The long-term game is about building adaptive capacity. You're building an organization that can recognize when something doesn't feel right and respond appropriately.

That means nurturing the human judgment that technology amplifies rather than replacing it. It means creating processes that can evolve as threats evolve. It means building a culture where verification is valued, skepticism is rewarded, and learning from mistakes is more important than avoiding them entirely.

Sometimes the best upgrade is better training on what you already have. Sometimes it's simplifying your processes rather than adding complexity.

Three years ago, most people had never heard of deepfakes. Today, they're a business-critical threat. Three years from now, the specific techniques and technologies will probably be completely different. But the underlying challenge—maintaining trust in a world where deception is increasingly sophisticated—will remain.

The organizations that thrive in that environment won't be the ones with the most advanced technology. They'll be the ones that best understand the balance between efficiency and security, between trust and verification, between human judgment and technological assistance.

Building that balance takes time. It takes patience. It takes a willingness to invest in capabilities that you hope you'll never need to use. But waiting until you're attacked to build your defenses is far more expensive than preventing them.

Your 90-day implementation is just the beginning. The real work happens in the months and years that follow, as you refine what you've built and adapt to what comes next. But if you've done the work outlined in this chapter—if you've built awareness, implemented systems, and created a culture of verification—you'll be ready for whatever comes next.

Because in the end, defending against deepfakes isn't really about the technology. It's about preserving something more fundamental: the ability to trust what matters while questioning what doesn't. And that's a skill worth developing, no matter what the future holds.

What's Next?

You've learned how to train your team to recognize deepfake manipulation and build a culture of verification within your organization. Your employees now have the skills to spot suspicious content and the confidence to question what they see and hear. But even the best-trained teams need to understand what they're preparing for.

In the next chapter, we'll look beyond today's threats to explore where deepfake technology is headed. You'll discover how AI avatars, quantum computing, and synthetic celebrities will reshape business, entertainment, and society itself. Understanding the future landscape of deepfake technology isn't just fascinating—it's essential for preparing your organization for the challenges and opportunities that lie ahead. The training you've implemented today will serve as your foundation for navigating tomorrow's synthetic reality.

Chapter 8

The Future of Deepfakes: Where This Is Headed

As deepfake technology continues to evolve, its impact on society, business, and communication will become more profound. What began as a tool for entertainment has now expanded into industries ranging from marketing to cybersecurity, leaving many to question where this technology will take us next. The rise of synthetic media presents both opportunities and threats, challenging how we perceive authenticity in a world where the line between reality and fabrication grows thinner by the day.

Throughout this book, you've seen how deepfakes evolved from grainy, uncanny images into sophisticated real-time illusions. But that's just the start. Today, a new generation of AI-driven tools like Google's Veo Suite and Runway ML are pushing the boundaries of what's possible. These aren't just your run-of-the-mill deepfakes; they're entire ecosystems of synthetic reality, enabling anyone to create cinematic-quality videos or images from a simple prompt. The ease of use and astonishing fidelity of these tools mark a new turning point, where creating an entirely fabricated scene can be done in minutes, not weeks.

This development is monumental because it transforms the long-standing traditions of visual storytelling. Only a few years ago, creating realistic visual effects required entire teams of artists, specialized equipment, and months of work at massive costs that could only be covered by major studios. On top of that, the gatekeepers of this craft, those with the technical expertise and access to high-end software, held a monopoly on who could create what. Now, those same tools are in the hands of anyone with a smartphone and an idea. An 80-year-old grandmother can create feature-level shots while sipping tea on her porch, turning personal visions into polished cinematic experiences. This sudden leap in accessibility and power hints at a world where the barriers to visual storytelling and the truth itself are vanishing faster than we ever imagined.

This chapter explores how these generative tools are reshaping the future of media itself. You'll look at how industries are adopting them, how artists are pushing boundaries, and how audiences are being asked to reimagine their relationship to what's real. This represents both a technical and cultural shift that redefines creativity, credibility, and the very idea of truth. Let's dive in and see what this new world looks like.

Generative Media: Uses and Consequences

Generative AI tools are revolutionizing marketing and advertising, empowering brands to create hyper-realistic deepfake videos and images that dazzle audiences and blur the lines between truth and fiction. These tools can conjure up synthetic faces, voices, and environments with ease, making them potent weapons in the fight for attention. The future of licensing our digital likenesses is uncertain, but one thing is crystal clear: owning your digital identity will soon be as important as owning your real one. This shift will fundamentally reshape how brands engage consumers and how creators protect their personal images. Yet marketers must tread carefully; in this new world of synthetic media, authenticity becomes both more valuable and more fragile, demanding ethical vigilance as never before.

Three-Dimensional Education

Educators will increasingly use generative media to create dynamic deepfake reenactments of historical figures and events. These tools will supercharge the classroom, making complex subjects not only more accessible but truly unforgettable. Imagine learning physics directly from Einstein himself or exploring math concepts alongside your favorite rapper, making every lesson more relatable and engaging. This newfound power will democratize access to creative teaching tools, but it must be wielded carefully to ensure accuracy and respect for likenesses and to prevent reinforcing biases or misinformation. As the estates of deceased individuals grapple with the use of their images, ethical stewardship will become more important than ever. We will even see the emergence of deepfake insurance companies to handle the misuse of likenesses and protect these digital identities in the future.

The Effect on "Real" News

The rise of deepfake technology is transforming journalism, offering ways to illustrate stories with synthetic visuals or voices that can bring a new level of dynamism and interactivity to reporting. However, this same power fuels the proliferation of fake news to levels we've never seen before. In the future, audiences will face an overwhelming challenge to distinguish what's real and what's not, forcing them to be more critical and skeptical than ever. Journalists will have to develop and adopt more rigorous verification techniques and perhaps even new standards of transparency and disclosure to combat the flood of faked audio and video content that threatens to completely erode public trust in media.

This echoes points made in previous chapters about the role of platforms and tech companies in controlling information flows. Although this kind of oversight can feel dystopian, the alternative—a total lack of oversight—would be far worse, opening the door to deepfake-fueled misinformation at unprecedented scale.

Creativity for the Masses

For creators, deepfake technology will be a powerful storytelling tool that signals the end of Hollywood's tight grip on media creation at scale and shifts power to independent artists and platforms. Indie filmmakers and digital artists will be able to seamlessly integrate actors into scenes or create lifelike performances that were previously out of reach. But deepfakes will also raise questions about consent, authenticity, and the ethics of manipulating reality in art. Although this is a win for the "little guy," it remains to be seen how much room there will be for this new and emerging segment in the shifting media landscape. Not to mention that this will need heavy policing to ensure that someone isn't using Tom Cruise for their short film without permission, akin to the Tom Cruise impersonator on TikTok that made the rounds on the Internet.

Determining the Truth

The proliferation of deepfakes across all these fields challenges our definitions of truth and trust. With deepfake videos and images growing more convincing, audiences are increasingly wary of what they see and hear. This forces a cultural reckoning: How do we preserve the integrity of media when even a video can be a lie? And what happens when different cultures begin using these tools to create negative portrayals of other cultures, stoking tension and conflict in ways we've never had to consider before? This represents a worldwide potential cultural divide, extending beyond American borders. In a world already rife with wars and civil unrest, people often look for reasons to justify their biases. All it might take is a single well-placed deepfake to ignite a bloody campaign in retribution for something that never even happened.

Avatars and Synthetic Celebrities

AI avatars are quickly becoming viable replacements for human presence in both personal and professional spaces. Imagine executives deploying AI versions of themselves to attend meetings, conduct negotiations, or deliver keynote addresses, all while they sit at home in their pajamas binge-watching old sitcoms. These digital clones, powered by deep learning, could analyze conversational patterns and decision-making habits to mimic their human counterparts with striking accuracy. In customer service, AI-driven representatives could interact with clients, providing seamless and automated assistance that feels indistinguishable from a real person. Although this technology could enhance efficiency and accessibility, it also raises ethical concerns. The more lifelike these avatars become, the harder it will be to distinguish a human from an AI-driven entity, which could lead to new challenges in trust and accountability.

These same challenges ripple through the world of AI-generated influencers and synthetic celebrities, where companies are already experimenting with entirely digital personalities, free from the unpredictability of human behavior. These AI-driven figures do not age, do not require breaks, and will never tweet something regrettable at 2 a.m. after a few too many drinks. Some argue that synthetic influencers will never truly replace human authenticity, but their rise signals a shift in how brands engage with audiences. If consumers begin to trust and interact with AI-generated figures as they would with real individuals, the traditional celebrity endorsement model may soon be obsolete.

Rewriting History

Beyond entertainment, one of the most significant concerns with deepfake technology is its potential to alter historical narratives. The ability to fabricate realistic videos of past events could reshape public perception of history, influencing everything from political discourse to legal cases.

The Future of Deepfakes: Where This Is Headed

The possibility of deepfakes being used to manipulate evidence or rewrite the past introduces new ethical dilemmas. If a video emerges showing a historical figure making statements they never actually said, how will future generations discern fact from fiction? Will textbooks come with a "may contain AI hallucinations" warning? (*AI hallucinations* refer to instances where models, especially large language models [LLMs], generate false or misleading information while presenting it confidently as fact.) The increasing sophistication of synthetic media requires society to develop new methods of verification, ensuring that truth is not easily rewritten by technological advancements.

The Future of Reality

As artificial intelligence becomes more ingrained in our daily lives, it will challenge traditional notions of reality. The concept of "post-reality" suggests that as deepfakes improve, people may begin to trust synthetic content over real-world experiences. In a world where AI-generated voices and videos become indistinguishable from genuine human interactions, will authenticity still matter, or will we all just start deepfaking our way through life, sending AI clones to do our taxes and break up with our significant others? Businesses, governments, and individuals will need to navigate this shift carefully, balancing innovation with ethical responsibility.

Technology continues to bring to life scenarios once confined to speculative fiction. The UK thriller *The Capture* portrays a chillingly realistic world where advanced surveillance systems and sophisticated manipulation of digital media fundamentally redefine our perception of reality. In the show, state-of-the-art video-altering technology, known as "Correction," seamlessly modifies real-time footage, creating compelling but entirely fabricated events. This tech allows operatives to frame individuals, alter narratives, and sway public opinion with near-perfect visual fidelity. Crucially, an official government agency uses this technology ostensibly for maintaining public safety and national security, confronting viewers with an intense moral dilemma: Is it acceptable to distort reality if it serves the greater good? The series highlights the ethical slippery slope of utilizing powerful tools, even for seemingly benevolent purposes, and questions who should wield such control over truth.

This ethical conundrum depicted in the show isn't merely speculative; it resonates deeply with the very patents and innovations Aliza contributed to, bridging the gap between fictional narrative and technological reality. These innovations raise profound questions about responsibility, power, and the potential consequences of their misuse.

Consider waking up to a frantic video call from your child studying abroad, pleading for emergency funds after a fabricated terrorist attack. Their voice, their expressions, flawlessly mimicked, exploiting your deepest fears. Or consider your company's virtual AI-driven conference call infiltrated by a malicious deepfake AI posing as a senior executive, authorizing massive financial transfers before anyone realizes it's a fraud.

At a state level, visualize a scenario where an AI-generated holographic candidate holds an incredibly realistic live-streamed town hall, captivating voters with emotionally charged rhetoric tailored precisely to local concerns. This candidate promises groundbreaking policy changes, like guaranteed universal income or revolutionary healthcare advancements, instantly galvanizing voter support. However, moments after securing victory, the hologram dissipates, leaving behind confusion, mistrust, and chaos, as citizens grapple with the realization they've been deceived by a nonexistent entity.

On an international scale, imagine a perfectly synchronized deepfake broadcast featuring multiple global leaders convincingly announcing coordinated military actions or drastic international policy shifts. These meticulously crafted messages appear simultaneously on major news networks, backed by AI-generated social media accounts and seemingly authentic official websites. This isn't future tech; it just hasn't happened yet. Within minutes, global stock markets spiral into chaos, triggering panic selling and financial collapse, while diplomatic hotlines overflow with frantic attempts to clarify and avert potential military conflicts. The careful orchestration and execution of such a campaign would exploit our global interconnectedness, swiftly destabilizing international relations before the truth can emerge.

Quantum Computing Speeds

What makes these futuristic threats particularly dangerous is their ability to infiltrate daily life unnoticed until it's too late. Our relationships, economies, and global stability will increasingly depend on distinguishing reality from illusion.

Enhanced by quantum computing speeds, these videos could propagate instantly through advanced AI-driven social media networks that tailor disinformation specifically to each viewer's biases and vulnerabilities. Quantum computing, which leverages the principles of superposition and entanglement to process massive datasets in parallel at speeds beyond classical computing, will pour nitroglycerin mixed with gasoline on these scenarios. It won't just accelerate deepfake creation; it will supercharge the precision of every pixel, every nuance of expression, and every algorithmic decision made. Quantum computing's ability to solve what once seemed like intractable problems means that synthetic media will be crafted and disseminated faster than we can comprehend, turning an already volatile landscape into an explosive cocktail of deepfake precision and algorithmic amplification. This will create an unstoppable wildfire of misinformation, fracturing communities and undermining trust at a fundamental level.

As quantum computing and AI-powered deepfakes become more intertwined, addressing these risks will require a two-pronged approach: top-down efforts by governments to regulate, legislate, and safeguard digital infrastructure, and bottom-up action by citizens who must remain vigilant, questioning what they see and hear.

Directing the Impact of Deepfakes

This begs a deeper question for every reader: How would you feel about letting your digital self, a carefully constructed AI mirror, interact with the world in your place? Would you be comfortable with an AI-driven version of you attending virtual meetings, delivering keynotes, or even appearing at graduations and family events while you remain physically elsewhere? Would you willingly allow your personal data and likeness to become a trusted stand-in for your presence? This is the crossroads we're approaching. It represents a profound redefinition of what it means to exist in a digitally fluid society, extending far beyond personal convenience or corporate productivity, and how much of ourselves we're willing to trade to stand in more than one place at once, to be everywhere and nowhere simultaneously, to let our digital twins speak for us in boardrooms and bedrooms alike.

It wasn't long ago when hopping into a stranger's backseat through a rideshare app felt like a social taboo, or when the arrival of driverless taxis like Waymo seemed like a distant sci-fi scenario. But these innovations quickly became normal, part of the everyday fabric of urban life. This chapter is no different. Although the idea of handing over parts of ourselves to synthetic versions of ourselves or allowing AI avatars to stand in for us at key life moments still feels as surreal as *Back to the Future II*, it's no longer science fiction. It's the next chapter of our human story, already unfolding, waiting for us to decide how much of ourselves we're willing to share with these digital shadows of reality.

The future of deepfakes encompasses both technological advancement and the choices we make. Like stepping into a stranger's car through a rideshare app or letting a driverless taxi guide us through traffic, these shifts seem daunting at first but become normalized as they integrate into our lives. Whether deepfakes enhance efficiency, redefine entertainment, or challenge historical integrity, the path forward depends on how society collectively chooses to wield this power.

What remains certain is that deepfakes are here to stay, and understanding their potential is crucial in preparing for the world they are shaping.

The question now is how comfortable we are in letting our digital selves blur the boundaries of our physical lives: attending events, speaking in our voices, and even rewriting the stories we tell about ourselves and each other.

Let's embark on this journey, stepping into the full humanity of it all and how it plays out in the modern day. We're confronted with a paradox: technology that can stand in for our presence but never truly embody our spirit. These tools can mimic our laughter, our cadence, and our facial expressions, but they cannot replicate the tangle of emotions, memories, and nuances that make us truly human. They lack the quiet moments of doubt, the hesitation that comes from caring deeply, the vulnerability of being seen in all our complexity. Yet here we are, inviting these digital reflections to walk alongside us, to speak in our voices, to become our stand-ins in a world that demands more from us than we can physically give. In the modern day, this is already happening in customer service chats, virtual influencers, and even family celebrations mediated by screens. We're navigating a new kind of intimacy and distance, learning to balance the convenience of digital presence with the ache for real human connection. In this space, we are challenged to ask ourselves:

What do we want from these digital companions? What are we willing to trade for the ease and efficiency they offer? And above all, how do we ensure that the spark of being alive, the unpolished, unfiltered, raw edges of our humanity, remains at the center of our lives even as our digital shadows grow ever more sophisticated?

The Growth and Adoption Cycle

Throughout the past 50 years, we've witnessed this cycle of introduction, resistance, and eventual growth unfold time and again. When personal computers first arrived, there was a mix of excitement and suspicion, and people wondered whether we truly needed them, whether they would change our lives or remain a niche luxury for tech enthusiasts. Meanwhile, skeptics worried about the dehumanizing effects of staring at screens for hours on end.

Then came the Internet: America Online's chirpy greeting; chatrooms where you could speak to strangers from around the world; IRC, or Internet Relay Chats, popular in the early days of personal computing, alive with global conversations. These spaces introduced us to the thrill of instant connection across distance, making the world feel smaller while making our lives feel bigger. Yet even then, there were concerns: would these digital communities replace the real ones, or just extend them in new ways? Soon they became indispensable, opening new realms of creativity and connection that once seemed out of reach. This technology upended the way we share information, build communities, and reimagine commerce.

Social media followed, starting with early platforms like GeoCities, Myspace, and blogs that allowed people to share their worlds in ways never seen before. These tools created new pathways for activism, friendship, and family ties that spanned continents. They opened the door to communities of shared interest, from political movements to fan-fiction circles, and made us realize the power of human connection in digital form. Each of these technological waves demanded that we confront our uncertainties, adapt our habits, and wrestle with how these tools would shape our daily lives. What once felt like alien intrusions soon became vital organs in our collective human experience, showing that although the first instinct may be to resist or fear, we have an uncanny ability to weave these tools into the very fabric of our existence, enriching it in ways we couldn't have imagined.

What's Next?

So what does this mean for individuals and businesses? It means that the very idea of authenticity is being redefined, and the stakes have never been higher. Businesses will need to develop robust systems for verifying their visual and audio communications—fact-checking isn't just for text anymore. Leaders will need to invest in technologies and partnerships that help distinguish real from synthetic content and make trust a competitive advantage.

Individuals, too, will have to sharpen their instincts. This means asking: Who created this content? Why does it exist? What motivations might be behind it? It means questioning first impressions, especially when something seems too perfect or too shocking to be real. It's about cultivating a healthy skepticism without sliding into cynicism.

For creators like me who work with these tools, the question becomes what we *should* make, beyond what we *can* make. We must hold ourselves to a higher standard, using these tools to amplify truth, not to obscure it. Because in a world where pixels can lie, intention is everything.

This moment calls on all of us to build new muscles of critical thinking and technical literacy. It's a turning point, one where we must balance the dazzling possibilities of generative media with the quiet but essential work of preserving trust. We must ensure that this technology serves both our imaginations and our values.

Over time, we've seen how technology moves from the fringes to the center of our lives. We adapted, learned to be cautious, and discovered new ways to connect, whether through AOL chatrooms or via the excitement of sharing a thought in a blog post. This history of adaptation and evolution provides the foundation for understanding our current technological moment. These tools are part of a long lineage of technology becoming part of our lives, an invisible companion that grows more capable and more deeply woven into our routines.

Working with the DMX estate showed me firsthand how this technology is both a gift and a responsibility. As a lifelong fan, I knew that re-creating his likeness was about the visuals as much as it was about capturing his spirit and energy, making sure it was done with care and respect. This work gently reminded me that deepfake tools are like gunpowder: they can create fireworks or launch bullets, depending on whose hands they're in. I feel a deep sense of caution about how easily accessible these tools have become. They're so powerful that if misused, they could be like ignoring a hole in a boat; by the time your ankles are wet, it may already be too late.

I'm not rejecting technology or fearfully turning away; I'm drawing a parallel between the history of technology and how we've interacted with it throughout time. Each new tool brings the same questions:

- How will it change us?
- How much of ourselves do we give to it?
- How do we ensure that we're using it to amplify what makes us human, not to replace it?

Just as we revisited the early examples of AI business applications, like avatars attending board meetings or handling customer service, we must see them as the natural next steps in this historical arc, not as threats in isolation. They tie back to the personal reflections and questions we're posing about comfort and digital self-extension. Just as we once learned not to share our real names or credit card information in chatrooms, or to be mindful of what we posted online, we now face a new frontier. The same caution—the same instincts to protect our identities and connections—applies here.

Again, I encourage you to reflect on your own experience and how you've grown alongside these advances, how you've learned to adapt, and how you might carry forward that same wisdom. I'm not asking for fear, but for awareness and thoughtful engagement. Because as much as these tools offer us new ways to connect, they also challenge us to remain grounded in our shared humanity. This is the new era of vigilance and opportunity, and it's ours to shape.

Chapter 9

CTRL+ALT+FAKE (Conclusion)

The journey through this book has been about more than just the mechanics of deepfakes and AI deception. It's been a reflection on trust, truth, and the fragile line between reality and illusion. As someone who stood at the forefront of this technology, witnessing both its exhilarating creative potential and its unnerving capacity for harm, I carry the weight of that duality.

There was a moment when I realized the technology I helped pioneer could be used in ways I never intended. That realization hit harder than any technical challenge I've faced. It made me question not just what I was creating but *why*. The weight of that question lingered long after the screen went dark, gnawing at the edges of my excitement for the technology. I felt an uncomfortable mix of pride and regret: pride in the innovation and regret in its potential misuse. It was like building a beautiful ship, only to realize that it could sail into dangerous waters without you at the helm. That realization forced me to confront my own role, not just as a creator but also as a gatekeeper of responsibility. The exhilaration of pushing boundaries suddenly collided with the sobering awareness of the boundaries I might have inadvertently erased. The rush of going viral, the thrill of bending reality—none of it compared to the sinking feeling of seeing similar tools manipulated for deceit. This is the reality we face: tools are neutral until they're not. That neutrality dissolves the moment human intention takes hold. I remember staring at a screen, watching a deepfake I didn't create—but I knew all too well how it was made. The face was perfect, the voice convincing, the lie seamless. It felt like looking into a mirror and seeing someone else staring back. That was the moment it hit me. This isn't just about technology; it's about trust and how easily it can be hijacked.

But this isn't a story of despair. It's a call to action. If we are to navigate this digital landscape, we need to sharpen our instincts and reclaim our critical thinking. Think of it like pressing CTRL+ALT+DELETE on your digital consciousness. Just as that key combination forces a computer to interrupt its current processes, assess what's running, and initiate a system reset, we need to interrupt our automatic responses, assess the information we're consuming, and reset our perceptions. It's about breaking the loop of passive consumption and reclaiming control over how we process and react to the digital world around us. It's time to reset. Reset your reality, your sense of security, and your relationship with skepticism:

- **Resetting your reality** means acknowledging that what you see and hear can no longer be taken at face value. We grew up trusting the evidence of our senses, believing that photographs, videos, and voices were unshakable proof of authenticity. That world is gone. Accepting this shift isn't about surrendering to paranoia; it's about adapting to a new normal. Imagine standing in front of a funhouse mirror. The reflection is distorted, but your brain knows something is off. That's the mindset to cultivate: not fear, but awareness. Awareness that what you see might not be the full story.

- **Resetting your sense of security** means redefining what it means to feel safe in the digital world. Security isn't just about strong passwords or firewalls anymore. It's about mental firewalls that act as filters that help you process information critically. In the past, security was about locking doors. Today, it's about questioning the person who claims to have the key. The most advanced security system in the world can't protect you from a convincing lie unless you're prepared to recognize it.

- **Resetting your relationship with skepticism** is perhaps the most crucial step. Skepticism isn't cynicism. It's not about distrusting everything; it's about not trusting blindly. Healthy skepticism is the ability to hold space for doubt, to pause before reacting, to ask, "What if this isn't true?" In an age where deception is packaged in high- definition and delivered with algorithmic precision, that pause is your superpower.

Consider the historical parallels. When the printing press was invented, it democratized knowledge but also spread propaganda. Radio brought voices into homes but amplified the reach of demagogues. Television showed us the world but filtered it through selective lenses. Each technological leap reshaped society's relationship with truth. We adapted then, and we can adapt now.

The power isn't in the algorithm; it's in the pause, that fleeting moment where you choose to question instead of react. When you see a video that triggers a strong emotion, stop and think. Ask yourself, "Does this seem too perfect, too outrageous, too tailored to provoke?" That pause is your first line of defense.

I was reminded of this power recently when I stumbled on an Instagram post claiming to reveal the "true inventor" of what we now know as the drone, specifically a four-motor multicopter. The post presented an AI-generated image, dressed up with just enough faux authenticity to seem plausible. Scrolling through the comments, I saw hundreds of people buying into it without question, celebrating the supposed historical revelation. Very few noticed the telltale signs that the image wasn't real. Because of my background, I could tell almost instantly that it was AI-generated. The details were off in subtle ways: textures too smooth, shadows that didn't quite make sense. It was like catching a glitch in the Matrix.

What hit me harder was when this same post resurfaced in a group conversation with friends. One of them mentioned it as if it were undisputed fact. He believed it to be irrefutable. When I pointed out that he'd been duped by a low-level AI scam, he didn't feel great about it. He admitted that he had some initial skepticism, but the overwhelming positivity in the comments and the way the image was presented eroded his doubt. This is exactly how disinformation spreads: not just through content but through the validation of others. The collective belief of a crowd can override individual instincts. This happens because people often seek social validation; when an idea is widely accepted, it creates a psychological safety net that diminishes doubt. The comfort of conformity can be more persuasive than personal skepticism, especially when reinforced by the positive reinforcement of others.

Verification becomes your shield:

- Simple techniques like reverse image searches can help identify if an image has appeared elsewhere online, often exposing its true origin.

- Cross-referencing facts with reputable news outlets, checking timestamps, and even analyzing metadata when available can provide critical context.

- Question inconsistencies in details such as lighting, reflections, or backgrounds in images—these subtle discrepancies often betray manipulated content.

- Don't rely on a single source. In a world where content spreads faster than truth can catch up, verification is more than a tool; it's a mindset. Dig deeper. Look for context, contradictions, and confirmations. The truth often hides in the details that most overlook.

- Share what you know. This battle isn't won in isolation. Start conversations. When you help others see the mechanics behind the illusion, you strip deception of its power.

Imagine a society where everyone has that mental firewall, where critical thinking is as instinctive as breathing. That's the future we can build together.

We're living in an era where reality can be replicated, manipulated, and sold back to us with frightening precision. But here's the truth. Technology evolves, but human resilience adapts. The key isn't in fearing the deepfake era. It's in outsmarting it. The threats are real, but so is our ability to counter them. With awareness, vigilance, and a commitment to truth, we can navigate this digital labyrinth. We can choose to be passive consumers or active participants in safeguarding reality.

For businesses, this goes beyond awareness and into action. Leaders must nurture a culture of verification and healthy doubt, encouraging teams to question and validate information before making decisions. Like cybersecurity, verification is not a one-time seminar or a checkbox. It is a daily practice, woven into every meeting and every strategy.

In a world where seeing is no longer believing, skepticism is more than a defense mechanism. It is the compass that guides us through the fog of digital deception. Trust it, refine it, and let it lead you to the truth.

Here are tangible next steps you can take to build that culture:

- First, encourage your team to ask questions and seek second opinions through a human, non-digital approach before accepting digital information.
- Second, provide clear channels for verifying facts, whether through trusted sources, fact-checking tools, or expert consultations.
- Third, make it a habit to pause and think before sharing or acting on information, setting an example as a leader.

These small, consistent actions can create a ripple effect, transforming how your organization navigates the digital world.

By weaving these practices into your daily operations, you build a culture of trust and critical thinking, where teams feel safe to question, confirm, and improve. This mindset becomes your strongest defense and your greatest asset in a world where truth is constantly tested. As I wrote in Chapter 1, when Myster Giraffe first showed me the power and peril of AI, I realized that one creative spark can shape the future.

I want to leave you with that same lesson: curiosity and verification are twin engines of progress and protection. When leaders embrace both curiosity and verification, they help their organizations see beyond the illusion and find the real story in the noise. That is how we stay ahead of deception and continue to lead with integrity.

Acknowledgments

Writing this book was never just about telling a story. It was about sharing the journey, with its laughs, its missteps, and the moments that shaped me into the person I am today. This was my first time writing a book, and I never considered myself to be an author. I was always curious, even as a child, wanting to know how things worked. I would take things apart, sometimes reassembling them. But I always appreciated the gift of creative freedom to explore and learn. I owe that debt of gratitude to my mother, who gave me the space to let my mind wander, turning the garage into my personal workshop. Like the ripples in a pond, that freedom led me to write this book.

This project was tough—tougher than I imagined. Inside your own head, everything makes sense, but trying to explain something that feels so innate is a real challenge. Thank you to Aliza for giving me the opportunity to crack the code with the help of an amazing team. Ken Lande, who provided structure and the logic I needed to keep moving forward, even when my ideas were swirling in a million directions. Maggie Katreva, who supported Aliza by bringing in work so we could show the world what we could do; Maggie wore so many hats: sourcing talent, planning shoots, and forecasting what was coming next. Dario Bertazoli and Anders Oland, the brilliant minds behind our ML models, who made sure our work was always cutting edge. And of course, Brian Lee, whose vision it was to create an army of digital influencers in the first place. He gave me the space to build and figure things out on favorable terms.

Thank you to my wife, Lauren, who let me ramble on about deepfake models crashing in the middle of the night, who only cared because she knew I did. To my sons, Carl IV and Maxwell, for being the lights in my life that give me a reason to make the world a better place for you to inherit. And to all my other friends and family who went on this journey with me—I'm immensely grateful for your patience and tolerance. It will never be forgotten.

Thank you to the Super Deepfake Squad: You showed me that the cutting edge can be as warm as it is sharp. And to every creator who has ever struggled to balance art and ethics, thank you for proving that the line is worth respecting.

Most of all, thank you to the readers with curious minds and skeptical hearts. You're the reason this story matters.

About the Author

Carl Bogan is a curious mind at heart, a seasoned creative technologist and an innovation consultant with more than 20 years of experience in visual effects, artificial intelligence, and real-time deepfake technology. As the creative force behind Myster Giraffe, Carl blends humor, pop culture, and technical wizardry to create deepfake videos that caught fire, captivating audiences and turning heads in the world of entertainment.

Known for his sharp eye as a VFX artist and his unwavering commitment to ethical AI stewardship, Carl has become a trusted voice in the conversation about deepfakes and digital deception. His work bridges the gap between art and science, blending technological mastery with a deep understanding of the cultural forces that shape how we see the world.

When he's not pushing boundaries with deepfake memes, Carl is exploring the next frontier of storytelling, developing and experimenting with new technologies, and always searching for the spark that connects us all.

Index

B

Beneath the Planet of the Apes,
42

Big Tech's role
  AI-generated celebrity
    scandal, 97
  boosting deepfake content,
    97
  identifying the boundaries,
    97–101
  internal verification policies,
    101
  profit from deepfake, 96
black swan problem, 73
Blogs, 5, 14, 163
British Journal of Photography,
37
brute-force method, 2, 3
business protection from
    liability, 137–140
ByteDance, 55

C

Call of Duty, 51
The Capture, 158
Cardi B/Will Smith mashup, 52,
    63, 74
A Christmas Carol, 16
cognitive dissonance, 1, 25

cognitive heuristics, 81
collective belief, 170
The Coming of the Fairies, 36
The Commissar Vanishes, 38
confirmation bias, 83
corporate fraud, 90, 111–112
corporate liability, 138
Correction state-of-the-art
    video-altering
    technology, 158
credibility testing of witness, 110
critical thinking, 24, 83, 140, 164,
    168, 171, 172
cultural anxiety, 47
cybercrime
  convincing video
    impersonation, 115
  erosion of trust, 113–114
  evolution of detection tools,
    119–120
  government responses,
    118–119
  lasting victim impact, 116–118
  phone-based scams, 112
  psychological vulnerability,
    115
  questioning the integrity, 115
  ripple effects, 114
  text-based scams, 112

D

coordinated military actions/
drastic international
policy shifts, 159–160
"Correction," 158–159
digital twins, 161
frantic video call, 159
growth and adoption cycle,
163–164
impact of deepfakes, 161–163
quantum computing speeds,
160–161
virtual AI-driven conference
call, 159
Princess Mary's Gift Book, 37
protest art, 75
public awareness campaigns,
101

Q
quantum computing, 160–161

R
r/deepfake subreddit, 5, 51
reality, resetting, 168
real-time deepfakes, 17–22,
92–94
real-time verification, 125–126
Reddit, 5, 51
Resemble AI, 51
retouching process, 40

ripple effects, 114, 172
Roomba Method, 2, 3
Runway ML, 153
Runway's Act-One, 55

S
sandboxing, 122
SawStop, 126–129, 131, 132
sense of security, resetting,
168–169
Sesame Street, 79–80
simple safeguards
cooling-off period, 135–137
personal code words, 133–135
Sinatra experiment, 19–21, 53
skepticism, 31, 83, 109, 112, 113,
116, 126, 135, 150, 164,
168–171
social media, 1, 3, 6, 41, 56, 83,
91, 94, 132, 163
Blogs, 14
Facebook, 52
fueling deepfakes, 101–103
Instagram, 5, 14, 15, 45
profits of Deepfake, 96–103
psychology, 23–25
TikTok, 54
Twitter/X, 14, 54
YouTube, 54
Space Ghost Coast to Coast, 16

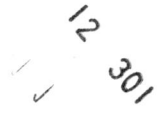

12 301